World of Dance

African Dance
Asian Dance
Ballet
European Dance
Middle Eastern Dance
Modern Dance

World of Dance

African Dance

Kariamu Welsh

CHELSEA HOUSE
PUBLISHERS
An imprint of Infobase Publishing

Frontispiece: Many African cultures emphasize specific gestures as part of their dance. For example, South African Zulus frequently use foot stomping as part of their performance.

African Dance

Copyright © 2004 by Infobase Publishing

Chelsea House
An imprint of Infobase Publishing
132 West 31st Street
New York NY 10001

ISBN-10: 0-7910-7641-5
ISBN-13: 978-0-7910-7641-5

Library of Congress Cataloging-in-Publication Data
Welsh, Kariamu.
   African dance/Kariamu Welsh.
      p. cm.—(World of dance)
   ISBN 0-7910-7641-5
   1. Dance—Africa. 2. Dance—Social aspects—Africa. 3. Dance, Black.
I. Title. II. Series.
GV1705.W43 2004
793.3'096—dc22   2004003392

Text and cover design by Terry Mallon

Printed in the United States of America

Bang 21C 10 9 8 7 6 5 4 3 2

This book is printed on acid-free paper.

Table of Contents

Introduction

Elizabeth A. Hanley
Associate Professor of Kinesiology, Penn State University

Dance has existed from time immemorial. It has been an integral part of celebrations and rituals, a means of communication with gods and among humans, and a basic source of enjoyment and beauty.

Dance is a fundamental element of human behavior and has evolved over the years from primitive movement of the earliest civilizations to traditional ethnic or folk styles, to the classical ballet and modern dance genres popular today. The term 'dance' is a broad one and, therefore, is not limited to the genres noted above. In the twenty-first century, dance includes ballroom, jazz, tap, aerobics, and a myriad of other movement activities.

The richness of cultural traditions observed in the ethnic, or folk, dance genre offers the participant, as well as the spectator, insight into the customs, geography, dress, and religious nature of a particular people. Originally passed on from one generation to the next, many ethnic, or folk, dances continue to evolve as our civilization and society change. From these quaint beginnings of traditional dance, a new genre emerged as a way to appeal to the upper level of society: ballet. This new form of dance rose quickly in popularity and remains so today. The genre of ethnic, or folk, dance continues to be an important part of ethnic communities throughout the United States, particularly in large cities.

When the era of modern dance emerged as a contrast and a challenge to the rigorously structured world of ballet, it was not readily accepted as an art form. Modern dance was interested in the communication of emotional experiences—through basic movement, through uninhibited movement—not through the academic tradition of ballet masters. Modern dance, however, found its aficionados and is a popular art form today.

No dance form is permanent, definitive, or ultimate. Change occurs, but the basic element of dance endures. Dance is for all people. One need only recall that dance needs neither common race nor common language for communication; it has been a universal means of communication forever.

The WORLD OF DANCE series provides a starting point for readers interested in learning about ethnic, or folk, dances of world cultures, as well as the art forms of ballet and modern dance. This series will feature an overview of the development of these dance genres, from a historical perspective to a practical one. Highlighting specific cultures, their dance steps and movements, and their customs and traditions will underscore the importance of these fundamental elements for the reader. Ballet and modern dance, more recent artistic dance genres, are explored in detail as well, giving the reader a comprehensive knowledge of their past, present, and potential future.

The one fact that each reader should remember is that dance has always been, and always will be, a form of communication. This is its legacy to the world.

❖   ❖   ❖

In this volume, Kariamu Welsh explores the varied dances of the world's second largest continent—Africa. Welsh divides the continent into four areas—west, east and central, north, and south—in detailing what the late anthropologist/choreographer/ dancer Pearl Primus referred to as "the soul of Africa." Dance in Africa is a pragmatic part of life. It celebrates the everyday events and occurrences in the lives of its people: rights of passage, the harvest, marriage, births, deaths, and historical events, among others. Dance is a political, religious, and social expression, and the quality of one's character is often judged through performance. From the masked dances of the west, to the Muslim-influenced dances of the north, to the Jerusarema of the south, dance will always be a reflection of life in Africa.

Foreword

Jacques D'Amboise
Founder, National Dance Institute

In song and dance, man expresses himself as a member of a higher community. He has forgotten how to walk and speak and is on the way into flying into the air, dancing. . . . his very gestures express enchantment.

—Friedrich Nietzsche

On Maria Dancing by Robert Burns

How graceful Maria leads the dance!
She's life itself. I never saw a foot
So nimble and so elegant; it speaks,
And the sweet whispering poetry it makes
Shames the musicians.

In a conversation with Balanchine discussing the definition of dance, we evolved the following description: "Dance is an expression of time and space, using the control of movement and gesture to communicate."

Dance is central to the human being's expression of emotion. Every time we shake someone's hand, lift a glass in a toast, wave goodbye, or applaud a performer—we are doing a form of dance. We live in a universe of time and space, and dance is an art form invented by human beings to express and convey emotions. Dance is profound.

There are melodies that, when played, will cause your heart to droop with sadness for no known reason. Or a rousing jig or mazurka will have your foot tapping in an accompanying rhythm, seemingly beyond your control. The emotions, contacted through music, spur the body to react physically. Our bodies have been programmed to express emotions. We dance for many reasons: for religious rituals from the most ancient times; for dealing with sadness, tearfully swaying and holding hands at a wake; for celebrating weddings, joyfully spinning in circles; for entertainment; for dating and mating. How many millions of couples through the ages have said, "We met at a dance"? But most of all, we dance for joy, often exclaiming, "How I love to dance!" Oh, the JOY OF DANCE!!

I was teaching dance at a boarding school for emotionally disturbed children, ages 9 through 16. They were participating with 20 other schools in the National Dance Institute's (NDI) year-round program. The boarding school children had been traumatized in frightening and mind-boggling ways. There were a dozen students in my class, and the average attention span may have been 15 seconds—which made for a raucous bunch. This was a tough class.

One young boy, an 11-year-old, was an exception. He never took his eyes off of me for the 35 minutes of the dance class, and they were blazing blue eyes—electric, set in a chalk-white face. His body was slim, trim, superbly proportioned, and he stood arrow-straight. His lips were clamped in a rigid, determined line as he learned and executed every dance step with amazing skill. His concentration was intense despite the wild cavorting, noise, and otherwise disruptive behavior supplied by his fellow classmates.

At the end of class I went up to him and said, "Wow, can you dance. You're great! What's your name?"

Those blue eyes didn't blink. Then he parted his ridged lips and bared his teeth in a grimace that may have been a smile. He had a big hole where his front teeth should be. I covered my shock and didn't let it show. Both top and bottom incisors had been worn away by his continual grinding and rubbing of them together. One of the supervisors of the school rushed over to me and said, "Oh, his name is Michael. He's very intelligent but he doesn't speak."

I heard Michael's story from the supervisor. Apparently, when he was a toddler in his playpen, he witnessed his father shooting his mother; then putting the gun to his own head, the father killed himself. It was close to three days before the neighbors broke in to find the dead and swollen bodies of his parents. The dehydrated and starving little boy was stuck in his playpen, sitting in his own filth. The orphaned Michael disappeared into the foster care system, eventually ending up in the boarding school. No one had ever heard him speak.

In the ensuing weeks of dance class, I built and developed choreography for Michael and his classmates. In the spring, they were scheduled to dance in a spectacular NDI show called *The Event of the Year*. At the boarding school, I used Michael as the leader and as a model for the others and began welding all of the kids together, inventing a vigorous and energetic dance to utilize their explosive energy. It took a while, but they were coming together, little by little over the months. And through all that time, the best in the class—the determined and concentrating Michael—never spoke.

That spring, dancers from the 22 different schools with which the NDI had dance programs were scheduled to come together at Madison Square Garden for *The Event of the Year*. There would be over 2,000 dancers, a symphony orchestra, a jazz orchestra, a chorus, Broadway stars, narrators, and Native American Indian drummers. There was scenery that was the length of an entire city block and visiting guest children from six foreign countries coming to dance with our New York City children. All of these elements had to come together and fit into a spectacular performance, with only one day of rehearsal. The foremost challenge was how to get 2,000 dancing children on stage for the opening number.

At NDI, we have developed a system called "The Runs." First, we divide the stage into a grid with colored lines making the outlines of box shapes, making a mosaic of patterns and shapes on the stage floor. Each outlined box holds a class from one of the schools, which would consist of 15 to 30 children. Then, we add various colored lines as tracks, starting offstage and leading to the boxes. The dancers line up in the wings, hallways, and various holding areas on either side of the stage. At the end of the overture, they burst onto stage, running and leaping and following their colored tracks to their respective boxes, where they explode into the opening dance number.

We had less than three minutes to accomplish "The Runs." It's as if a couple of dozen trains coming from different places and traveling on different tracks all arrived at a station at the same time, safely pulling into their allotted spaces. But even before starting, it would take us almost an hour just to get the dancers lined up in the correct holding areas offstage, ready to make their entrance. We had scheduled one shot to rehearse the opening. It had to work the first time or we would have to repeat everything. That meant going into overtime at a great expense.

I gave the cue to start the number. The orchestra, singers, lights, and stagehands all commenced on cue, and the avalanche of 2,000 children were let loose on their tracks. "The Runs" had begun!

After about a minute, I realized something was wrong. There was a big pileup on stage left and children were colliding into each other and bunching up behind some obstacle. I ran over to discover the source of the problem—Michael and his classmates. He had ignored everything and led the group from his school right up front, as close to the audience as he could get. Inspiring his dancing buddies, they were a crew of leaping, contorting demons—dancing up a storm, but blocking some 600 other dancers trying to get through.

I rushed up to them yelling, "You're in the wrong place! Back up! Back up!"

Michael—with his eyes blazing, mouth open, and legs and arms spinning in dance movements like an eggbeater—yelled out, "Oh, I am so happy! I am so happy! Thank you Jacques! Oh, it's so good! I am so happy!"

I backed off, stunned into silence. I sat down in the first row of the audience to be joined by several of the supervisors, teachers, and chaperones from Michael's school, our mouths open in wonder. The spirit of dance had taken over Michael and his classmates. No one danced better or with more passion in the whole show that night and with Michael leading the way—the JOY OF DANCE at work. (We went into overtime but so what!)

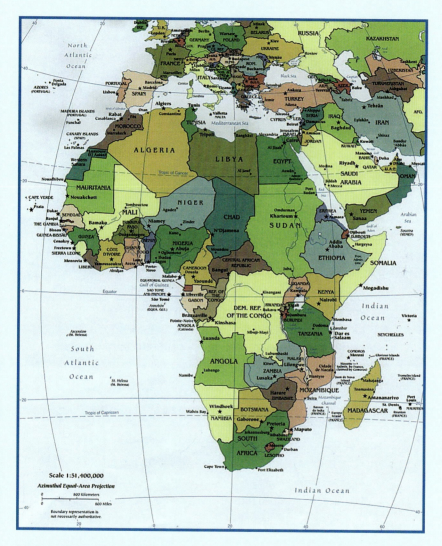

Africa consists of 54 countries and is the second largest continent in the world. With its thousands of cultures and languages, along with its varied geography, Africa has cultivated a wide range of dances.

1

Dance as a Reflection of Life

Africa is a continent with 54 countries and thousands of cultures and languages. Dance in Africa is a holistic part of society. It is not truncated or separated as an entity in and of itself. Dance is used to facilitate all phenomena in most African societies. All commemorations and events are documented in the dance. Births, deaths, weddings, corona- tions, and rites of passages are just some of the occasions for which dance is performed. Other events that dance chronicles are celestial occurrences, harvest times, fertility rites, and healing circles.

The kinds of dances vary but generally fall under the following categories: stilt dances; mask dances; military, war, and martial arts dances; rites-of-passage dances; harvest dances; story and myth dances; social and ceremonial dances; funeral dances; ancient court dances; work dances; healing dances; religious and spiritual dances; and, national- and ethnic-identity dances. Some of these categories overlap and are not mutually exclusive.

Stilt dances are performed throughout Africa. A dancer balances on long wooden stilts that vary in height. The stilts are covered with the same fabric of the dancer's costume to give the illusion that the dancer has extremely long legs. Even on stilts, the dancer performs various acrobatic feats, such as jumping rope. In addition, stilt dancers are often seen as the protectors of a village, as their heightened appearance lends itself to being the village guardian.

Mask dances performed throughout Africa are used in a variety of ways, including: warding off evil spirits; story-telling; suggesting supernatural or mystical powers; spreading good feelings; honoring African deities; and/or embodying animal, human, or spiritual figures. Some mask dances have a figure who is disguised with a painted face and body covering, while others use a facial mask and elaborate head-dress. The ornamentation of the mask figure aids in serving the varied purposes of the dance, yet the element of disguise is pervasive throughout.

For the most part, in traditional settings, military, war, and martial arts dances are performed by men, but there are exceptions in some ethnic groups where women participate in or have their own war dances. The dancers stylize their movements to depict war and conquest. Often the prowess of the person is depicted in dance through strong, athletic movements or intricate footwork.

The rites-of-passage dances or initiation dances often represent a child or adolescent's transition or even transfor-mation into early man or womanhood. The dances range from detailed footwork all the way to a swinging of the hips. The aesthetic qualities of the dances vary greatly by ethnic group. These dances often are more than just figurative representa-tions and, for many ethnic groups, suggest an actual change in status from childhood to manhood or womanhood.

In Africa, there is a deeply held respect for the earth. This is particularly evident in the harvest dances where the dances express thankfulness for the fruits of the earth, a hunger that is of the past, and a purification of the ground and water. Often songs are used to accompany these dances in homage to farming and the earth.

Storytelling is the major component of story and myth dances. The dances metaphorically tell the story of an important historical or current event, often with humor and a sense of awe. The purpose of the dances is to reenact a historical event; honor a deity figure or the heroic deeds of the deceased; and even to quell antisocial behavior. Singing is often performed. The songs either serve as an accompaniment to the story and myth dances or they are performed as an actual part of the story.

Social and ceremonial dances are performed in both traditional and contemporary settings, such as a nightclub. Social dances are performed to popular music, which often has political and ethnic themes, and for pure entertainment. Ceremonial dances are performed by men and women at various celebrations and festivals.

Funeral dances are performed throughout Africa, although some ethnic groups do not have dancing at burial rites. The dances that are performed signify the ethnicity, gender, and social status of the deceased. The dress that is worn by each ethnic group entails a wide range of colors, textures, and ornamentation.

Court dances are often rooted in precolonial eras in the kingdoms of both male and female African rulers; unfortunately, little is known about them because of European colonization. Work dances figuratively suggest a man or woman carrying out various occupational tasks, such as the hammering of the blacksmith, the action of meat sellers, or the work of fishermen casting nets and using spears and fish traps. Healing dances were performed to purify and clean an individual or community of people. Often the dances invoked an African deity who the

Nigerian dancers celebrate Durbar. Originally a military parade to honor the Emir of Nigeria, the dance is now celebrated during the Muslim festivals of Id-el Fitri and Id-el Kabir, and to honor visiting heads of state.

people identify as possessing the power to heal. Religious and spiritual dances are designated as those that are specifically performed to pay homage to a deity. National and ethnic dances are designated as those that show allegiance to one's national and ethnic background performed to songs that speak to national strength and loyalty.

All African dances can be used for transcendence and transformation purposes. Transcendence is the term usually associated with possession and trance. Dance is the conduit for transcendent activities. Dance enables an initiate or practitioner to progress or travel through several altered states, thereby achieving communication with an ancestor or deity and receiving valuable information that he can relay back to the community. Repetition is key to this process as it guides the initiates or dancers through the process of the ceremony. The more a movement is repeated, the greater the level of intensity and the closer the dancer gets to the designated deity or ancestor. Transformation is to change from one state or phase to another.

African dance can be defined as a collection of dances that are imbued with meaning, infused purposely with rhythm, and connected to the ritual, events, occasions, and mythologies of a specific people. African dance is theater in that it involves song, drama, masquerade traditions, and music. In this book, African dance is discussed from a historical and traditional perspective, i.e., the dances mentioned represent ancient and past traditions that may not be operative, applicable, or even viable today. These dance traditions provide a foundation for contemporary expressions. Generalizations about African dance as an absolute are inappropriate and inaccurate. It is useful for the purposes of this book to speak about African culture as an entity. This simply means that these dances originate in Africa and share cultures where traditionally dance is integral to and central to the society. This book acknowledges and appreciates the differences and contradictions that exist in and among the many cultures that are discussed throughout.

African dance can be classified by the following styles: Traditional, Neotraditional, and Stylized. Traditional dances are those dances that embody the cultural values of a particular society, are acknowledged as being of that society, and adhere to specific customs and rituals. Neotraditional dances are those dances that are created in the spirit or likeness of traditional dances but do not necessarily come from that particular society and, as a result, are not bound to all the aesthetic and cultural rules of that society. Classical dance in general can be defined as representing the best aesthetic ideals of a particular society; recognition of the dance by the masses; and formal or institutionalized instruction either in the courts, by private instruction, or communal learning vis-à-vis festivals. It is generational and time honored. Some examples of classical African dances are Lamban, Lindjien, and Sabaar from the Senegambian, Guinea, and Malian regions; and Fanga from Liberia, Adowa from Ghana, and Odunde from Nigeria.

Dancing in Africa developed as an essential, functional part of life. Every important event—birth, death, harvest, and marriage—is commemorated by dance. Dancing is a major part of festivals to thank the deities for a bountiful harvest. Other African dances celebrate the passage from childhood to adulthood. These dances are almost always gender-specific, with boys dancing with boys and girls dancing with girls. There are, of course, social dances in which courtship, flirtation, and socializing are encouraged and enjoyed. Many dances that were originally harvest or fertility dances have now become social dances as the society changes and the functions of those dances are no longer relevant or germane to the people. The dance, however, survives and takes on new meaning.

Dance worldwide is an effective means of communication and it is no different in Africa. The ability to express oneself without speaking is treasured in many traditional societies in Africa. Ideas can be conveyed that the entire community can understand and appreciate in such a way that dance affirms the community and its culture and history. Through dance, a group can regulate or monitor the social behavior of individuals by expressing approval or disapproval. The dance is part of the cultural expression. Performance usually includes some type of dramatic presentation, music, costume, song, and mask. The movement is central to the activity, but it is by no means the sum total of the event.

Dance is one of the world's oldest art forms. It is a mercurial art form: It exists in the moment, and, while a dance can be performed repeatedly, each performance is distinct and unique. Because of its ephemeral nature—in that it exists only in the moment—dance is cherished as it is performed. Dance is a dynamic art, transferring energy and consuming space in a way that fires and intrigues the imagination of the audience. Dance is exciting, it is physical, and it is almost always inseparable from music. People dance to express themselves and the body is the chief vehicle for that expression.

Dance is traditionally a communal and social activity. Rituals and ceremonies are often centered on the dance. In this way, dance is more than entertainment: it is an integral part of a society's worldview. A worldview is the way in which a person or group makes sense of its relationship with nature, God, or a supreme being. Dance is an expression. It expresses in movement and rhythm the aesthetic values of a society. Aesthetic values are the aspects of society that are perceived to be beautiful and indicative of the best of that society. The perception of one's environment and its relationship with nature is an important part of an aesthetic. Geography, religion, and gender are a few of the influences on dance. Different cultures emphasize particular parts of their bodies based on their belief systems, environment, and physical structures. For example, Ethiopian men articulate their shoulders in a thrusting, powerful gesture of masculinity, virility, and strength, while other cultures emphasize specific movements.

The South African Zulus are known for their foot-stomping movements that send the dust flying and create a resonating force that can be felt through the ground. The vertical jumps of the Masai people of Kenya and Tanzania reinforce and embellish the tall, lanky stature of the people. Many dances are performed only by males or females, indicating strong beliefs about what being male or female means and strict taboos about interaction.

The history of Africa dates back more than 3,000 years and scholars have documented dance from those earliest beginnings in ancient Egypt or Kemet (as it was once called). On the walls of caves in Algeria, on ancient Egyptians' papyri (written scroll), and on rocks in the caves of the San people in southern Africa, we find images of people dancing, which confirms the importance of dance in early human civilizations. Sometimes dance transcends languages and borders; other times dance is confined to secret societies and customs that prohibit it from being performed in public.

The late anthropologist/dancer Pearl Primus spoke eloquently about African dance: "Dance is the soul of Africa. It is the foundation of all of the arts and it weaves a tale about the daily lives of the people." In other words, African dance facilitates all phenomena in Africa. African dance is a multidimensional, multiperspective discipline that has impacted many areas in the humanities. Geoffrey Gorer's *African Dances*, written in 1934, was one of the first books to focus on African dance. Gorer chronicles his travels through Africa with remarkable description and detail, and the book is invaluable in this regard if one understands the time and context in which it was written. Many early writings on African dance were descriptive but, unfortunately, portrayed Africans in stereotypical and often biased ways. Missionaries, traders, and colonial administrators did not understand the dances that they were viewing and interpreted the dance through their

The late anthropologist/dancer/choreographer Pearl Primus was known for her virtuoso performances, which often combined African-American, Caribbean, and African dance with modern dance and ballet.

worldview, which saw the dances as antithetical to what they considered to be civilized behaviors.

African dance portrays the beliefs and value systems of its people. African dance traditions are expected to express moral values; their beauty and power lie in the expression of these values through movements. Skilled execution includes the ability to make the work beautiful by means of artistic devices, such as dynamism, energetic movements, accompanied songs and rhythms, drums and other percussive instruments, as well as the virtuosity of the individual. Given the nature and magnitude of African dance, it is important to remember that there are exceptions and contradictions that defy definition, classification, and documentation. It is impossible for any book to adequately or fully discuss the enormous topic of African dance and this book is no exception. This is an introduction to African dance that highlights selected dances from each region and provides an overview of some foundational aspects of African dance, as it relates to history, culture, and aesthetics.

In Africa, dance is performed for social, political, and religious reasons. In this way, dance has an impact on all institutions in society. The pervasive quality of dance in African societies is indicative of its importance in the daily lives of Africans. African dance can provide insight into gender roles and relationships, religions and belief systems, ceremonies, age-group relationships and expectations, and celebrations and relationship with nature.

African dance is not only entertainment; it is an introduction to African culture and customs. The information that one can receive about the various societies can be useful in studying and appreciating African cultures. In the present global climate where multiculturalism is encouraged, dance can play an important part in opening up new areas of knowledge, appreciation, and tolerance.

In many parts of Africa, one must be of good character to participate in dance. The dancer and the drummer are evaluated within the context of the society. Any person recognized as immoral or bad could not possibly uphold, display, or demonstrate the community's most treasured

A Kenyan performs a traditional dance while beating a drum. The connection between character and skill is important in African society, and dancers and drummers are held in high esteem.

dances, regardless of their natural abilities. An outstanding performance is a reflection of a person's high moral character. This connection between character and skill is an important one, and is indicative of the holistic way in which many Africans see each other. Behavior is not isolated from other spheres in one's life, such as performance. It is incongruous to the traditional African worldview that one can be evil and dance well.

Achievement and skill are sought after and worked for, but the process in African dance is just as important as the end product. Perfection is not the ideal in African dance; rather it is the culmination of the dancer's skill meshed with the musician's rhythms and his or her understanding of the overall event that makes the performance admirable or memorable. Excellence is a goal and is greatly appreciated but not at the expense of the dancer, other dancers and musicians, and/or the ritual.

Time, space, and rhythm all converge to create the dynamics of African dance. Many characteristics of African dance forms embody a particular worldview or stance that is informative about that society. For instance, Dogon men of Mali dance an elaborate dance in which they swing tall helmet masks in large circular patterns along the ground. The prowess and skill of the men illustrate the Dogon's dependence on rain for the harvesting of the crops. This dance is an appeal or prayer for rain. The more powerful the thrust and swings of the masks, the Dogon people believe, the greater the likelihood of rain.

MYTH: THE FOUNDATION OF DANCE

Myth is the foundation of many celebrations in Africa because it gives the ceremony or event its purpose. Many myths are based on the idea of a "creation story"; it relates how something was produced, created, or originated. Every society has a creation story that helps to explain how that society came about. For the Dogon people, the Tyi Wara, a mythical creature—half antelope, half man—is believed to have come down to earth to teach the Dogon people how to cultivate the earth. There is a dance to commemorate the Tyi Wara, and this is an example of how mythology is manifested in a dance.

The assignment of roles and responsibilities, especially of royalty, men, and women, is the subject of many a story or tale. These stories are designed to instruct the community on leadership and citizenry, and to serve as a cautionary tale for those who would stray.

An example of the prominence of dance in all spheres of African society is the transition between kings. A king in the Luba tribe of Congo did not want to abdicate his throne to a favored young man, so he devised a trap for the would-be king. There was a designated place in the center of the village where the king would dance before handing over his title. The king had his subjects dig a hole under the dancing ground and install daggers into the hole that pointed upwards. The plan was to have the heir to the throne go to the dancing ground, and when he danced, he would fall into the hole of daggers and kill himself. Essentially, the dance was a strategic instrument for the control of the community. Members of the king's court alerted the young man to the plot, and he skillfully danced around the hole of daggers. The king was forced by tradition to give over the kingship to the young heir apparent. It was and is expected of every king, chief, and ruler that he or she is able to dance.

In Ghana, the Asantehene, the paramount ruler of the Ashanti people, has to dance in front of the community before he can assume the role of Asantehene. This is not merely a symbolic gesture; rather it is a test of the man's commitment to and respect for the culture, and consequently his commitment to the people. The dance represents tradition and continuity in the Asante community. The preceding generations of Asantehenes danced the same dance, and it is their energy that the incoming Asantehene must draw upon. If the man cannot dance, he must learn to dance, and it is the responsibility of his court to teach him well. There is no waiver of this requirement to dance. The dance must be danced!

African dance in the context of African culture is the most transitory and fluid of the arts and resists documentation because of its ethereal and ephemeral qualities. Time is an important element when looking at any dance. In the case of African dance, many traditional dances could continue for days. The dance was part of a ceremony or ritual and went on as long as the demands of the occasion dictated. The length of a dance is not predetermined and since it is usually contained in a ritual, festival, or ceremony, the duration of the dance is not important. The beginning of a dance and its end are determined by the event, and as a consequence, the dance is responsive to the environs of the festival or ritual. The dance ebbs and flows and even stops periodically, but it is contained within the ceremony or ritual, and as long as the ceremony or ritual lasts, the dance lasts. Dance is a much more ephemeral art than either plastic arts or music; consequently, it has been difficult to document and its survival has depended on the dance being passed down from generation to generation. The oral tradition has been instrumental in keeping the traditions of African dance alive. This word-of-mouth phenomenon extends to the body as well and just as the stories are passed down from one generation to another, so are the dances.

The introduction of African art forms to the audiences of Europe and America in the early twentieth century changed the way in which Europeans looked at their own art and the cultures of African people. Pablo Picasso, among other plastic artists, adopted African abstraction in the early part of the twentieth century. It was this African influence that brought European art from its impressionistic and realistic stages to the development of abstraction as a major form of art. By observing and studying the abstractions of African sculptures, the European modern masters were able to find new modes for the expression of their emotions. What these masters failed to realize was that most African sculptures are dance masks. The sculptures are of the same rituals that dances are. These sculptures are organic, dynamic, and, more importantly, active parts of a tradition that empowers the mask once someone dons one.

African dance has been influenced in the world in much the same way as African art. The qualities of polyrhythm and total body articulation have found their way into modern dance forms as well as jazz dance and social dances like hip-hop. African dance has been performed at the World's Fair ever since the late 1800s. When many African nations gained their independence in the late 1950s and 1960s, one of their first acts was to create national dance companies that would showcase the best of their dances and to send these companies abroad to promote African culture.

African dance is fluid and mobile. For instance, the Yoruba people primarily live in Nigeria; however, there is also a thriving Yoruba community in Benin, so dances can reflect Yoruba culture but come from two different nations. The same can be said of the Ngoni people of East Africa. Ngoni live in Kenya, Tanzania, and Malawi as well as in many countries of southern Africa. The Ngoma dance that is danced in Kenya bears the same name and origin of the dance that is danced in Tanzania, but it has taken on the particular and specific history and culture of Kenya.

In 1884, the Berlin Conference was held with the intention of ending the slave trade and promoting humanitarian efforts in Africa. Instead it separated ethnic groups and nations into nation-states that disregarded the previous groupings and consequently ignored historical and cultural realities that the reconfigured states could not duplicate. The newly constituted regions created divisions based on ethnicity and cultures within the confines of a nation-state that was not always compatible. For the purposes of this book, Africa is divided into four geographical areas in order to organize the dances and to focus on some of the main traits and characteristics of the selected region. The four areas are west, east and central, north, and south. These divisions help the reader locate the dances but do not necessarily reflect the political, religious, historical, ethnic, or social divisions of the regions.

CHANGE AND TRANSITION

Many African dances have become multifunctional as a result of urbanization and secularization. Rural areas remain the citadels of culture, as they are often home to some of the oldest members of the community. In addition, the rural areas have not been as exposed to outside influences as the cities and metropolitan areas, and they are able to retain cultural practices. The rural areas also provide an environment that encourages the learning, teaching, and practicing of the dances. Space, flexibility and leisure time, the presence of elders, and a close community are just some of the features that the rural areas are able to contribute and provide an arena for the preservation of traditional dances. These influences are manifested namely by the exodus of so many young people to the cities and the periodic return of these people who bring with them changes, new influences, and different perspectives on what had once been an unquestioned and unchallenged part of life. The following is an example of three widely performed dances that now represent different things to the same people.

DANCES AND THEIR MEANINGS

DANCE	REGION	MEANING OF DANCE
Mandiani	Mali, Burkina Faso, Gambia, and Senegal	Wedding dance, dance of celebration, and rites-of-passage dance
Muchongoyo	South Africa, Mozambique, Zimbabwe, Lesotho, and Swaziland	Military training, dances of the diamond mines, festivals, and competitions
Geerbol	Niger, Mali, and Sudan	Annual rest of the Wodaabe nomads, courting dance, and celebration of the new year.

African dance is flexible and dynamic. This quality has enabled the dance to survive internal and external changes. African dance is able to absorb influences without losing its cultural identity and signature. The people are able to maintain the movements with their energy, form, and structure of the steps. What does affect the dance is the time element, which is greatly reduced as increased urbanization impinges on the duration of the dance, which traditionally can last for days. Another change is the presentation and participation in the dance. The dance is usually performed as a communal event with everyone participating. There is no audience per se but rather an interchangeable arrangement that allows dancers to ebb and flow into the dance, and to change roles and play instruments. There is no fixed part of the event and the musicians can quickly change and play another role. In contemporary times, traditional dance has been used to entertain dignitaries and heads of states and celebrate national holidays, which has had a great impact on the dance. Traditional dances are used for these occasions in ways that require changes in presentation. The dancers must adhere to a strict time limit and the performance is frontal without any interaction between the dancers and the audience. These changes make the dances remarkably different from their original incarnation.

MUSIC AND DANCE—ONE AND THE SAME

"We are almost a nation of dancers, musicians, and poets," remarked Olaudah Equiano, an African intellectual and explorer who lived in the eighteenth century. Religion played a central role in the lives of West Africans and the music, dance, and other arts reflected those belief systems. In Africa, the religious ceremonies used music and dance to help people make spiritual connections to their ancestors. Dance is music and music is dance in African cultures. The two are inseparable and in many African languages, there is not a separate word for dance.

Musicians were admired for the skill with which they played their drums, whistles, horns, guitars, flutes, and other instruments in complicated rhythms. A favorite kind of music had a call-and-response pattern. The leader sang out a short bit of music and the people sang it back to him, accompanied by drums and other percussion instruments.

The late Ghanaian dancer, scholar, and teacher, Alfred Mawere Opoku, in his discussion of dance as an art form in African cultures, articulates its organic relationship with music. Dance to the African, he writes, "is a language and a mode of expression" which articulates "special and real-life experiences in rhythmic sequence to musical and poetic stimuli." He goes on to say, "those who drum, dance, clap and sing together are the children of love and the drum is their mother."

The African art scholar Robert Farris Thompson also notes: "dance and music are very closely interwoven in African cultures." Dance facilitates all phenomena and provides a link to both the ancestral world and the divine world. African dance requires a musical sophistication in order to adequately participate within the rhythmic framework of a particular movement. In the article "Commonalities in African Dance," I make the statement that "the rhythmic sense as an aspect of polyrhythm is evident in all disciplines; particularly in the marriage of music and dance where the sacred circle joins the two." According to Opoku, the druming, singing, and clapping play an equally important "role in the drama of African community life. They set the scene, create the mood and the atmosphere" for the dancer to interpret music through symbolic gestures, bodily movements, and facial expression.

Dancing and drumming are rich artistic activities that play central roles in many traditional cultures in Africa. African dance and drum traditions are two distinct expressions of the same entity: rhythm. Both dancing and drumming require accompaniment. Dancing demands physical involvement, while drumming demands human participation. In other words, the use of the human body is required in both dancing and drumming. Rather than the material separation of the arts from each other and the physical distinctions between the played and the player, African culture relies upon a holistic integration that encourages the collective and the communal.

As a real and rational entity, rhythm is permanently ensconced in a tradition that is dynamic and vital. If one is able to conceptualize rhythm as text, then both dance and drumming can be viewed as two sides of the same coin. Text then provides structure that is dynamic and documentable. Unlike written text, dance as text is distinguished by its oral quality, even when it is manifested as visual, kinetic, or sensory. Contextually, dancing and drumming are the same. Although perceived differently, they both emanate from the same foundation, namely rhythm. There are many distinctions and differences to be sure, but those distinctions are internal and interrelated within the African dance body.

For instance, if one looks at the Soba dance, the approach can vary according to what is being observed. What is constant, however, is the idea that the Soba is the sum total of its movements and rhythms. Rhythm remains the central core to any expression of African culture. Let's take Soba again as an example. This particular dance is from Senegal, a country in West Africa. It is also a traditional dance, meaning that it is generational and recognizable by the community. Soba is a rites-of-passage dance in that young women who were making a transition from girlhood to womanhood originally performed it. This transition had more to do with preparation for marriage and motherhood than anything else. How to describe Soba then? It can be recognized by its steps but never confused with just being them! It can be acknowledged by its dancers, but never confuse the dancers with the dance! It can be witnessed by its rhythms but, again, never be defined as just music! Rhythm acts as the pervasive and identifying agent in both African dance and music.

In most cases, the rhythm identifies the text as well as the context. The community recognizes Soba by its rhythm. The intensity of a rhythm signals precisely where the entire community should focus its attention. The rhythm also assists in identifying who is present, particularly the presence of dignitaries, strangers, and spirits. The movements themselves do not change, but the rhythm provides the framework that instructs and informs the choreography, the performers, and the audience. This structure allows for an optimal freedom of expression, and yet maintains the continuity of tradition and dynamics in place.

To further understand African culture, African music and dance rhythm have to be at the center of any analysis. Consequently, all research must focus on the text in a variety of ways. First, the text of the ritual must be examined, then the text of the music must be examined, and then the text of the dance. While the words themselves represent distinct functions of rhythm, they are often used interchangeably with rhythm. The confusion indicates the fine line between dance and rhythm, and between music and rhythm.

Rhythm enhances the artistic consciousness of the artist and performer. It renders new and different meanings each time, thereby opening new dimensions in creativity. The fact is that rhythm is both a powerful and subtle aspect of the African arts. Although rhythm has been subjected to numerous inter-pretations and theories, none of them sufficiently explains the phenomena; the real understanding is to understand that each time a meaning is discovered, there remains another meaning to be uncovered. Rhythm emphasizes the African worldview and when applied to dance it is a visual illumination of that particular worldview. Additionally, it serves to highlight its ambiguities and contradictions as well as incongruities by irregular and off-centered rhythms. Rhythm emanates from both the performer's and the observer's worldview thereby contrasting and affirming the entire community's perception of the event.

GENDER ISSUES

Women use dance to convey modesty, grace, and demureness—
often to express gender identity. In addition, all through Africa,
a woman's ability to bear children is central to her identity
and this is reflected through the numerous initiation dances
throughout Africa that usher her into adulthood. A woman's
childbearing abilities and her subsequent bearing of children
are central to her position and status in her community. Dance
is one of the conduits for young women to learn and prepare
for motherhood.

AESTHETICS

Dances are polyrhythmic, meaning that many rhythms are
occurring at the same time and the dancers are able to dance
to those rhythms and switch back and forth between rhythms
without missing movements. Dances are generally performed
barefoot except in the case of many southern African dances
where boots and shoes are often used because of the region's
history of men working in the gold mines, and thus dances were
created as a result of that experience. Body isolation is common
in many African dances, with one part of the body being
expressly articulated. In the Egyptian Baladi dance (commonly
known as the belly dance), it is the abdomen; in the Zimbabwean Jerusarema, it is the legs and the hips; in the Ghanaian
Adowa, it is the hands; and in the Benin Beni, it is the arms.
The emphasis on specific body parts is directly linked to geographical and religious influences. In the southern African
region, the striking of the legs into the earth is very prevalent as
the earth is dry and the goal many times is to send the dust flying
as a way of demonstrating the force and power of the movement.
In countries where Islam is influential or dominant, hand
gestures are favored as a means of expression. African dances
in general tend to be grounded, with the focus toward the earth.

The earth is revered in most African cultures because that
is where the ancestors reside and the earth is the repository

of the food for the people. African dances are dynamic in ways that challenge rhythmic sensibilities. The dynamics are engineered to give the dances texture and to elevate or transcend the material or physical world. In other words, for African dance, speed and repetition aids and facilitates transcendence, which is often a desired goal. African dance is largely participatory, meaning that the spectators are a part of the performance as well. Traditionally, there are no rigid barriers between dancers and the onlookers unless it is a spiritual, religious, or initiation dance. Even when a dance is specifically performed for a ritual, there is often a time in the dance when people may join in and then leave at a designated time. Spectators become the dancers and dancers become the spectators in many social and celebratory dances. This is effective in ensuring that everyone in the community dances and not just a few elite. Good dancers are valued as they are in any society, but the right to dance belongs to everyone. In this way, dancers of all ages are facilitated, included, and represented at the event. Very young children and the elderly are revered for their dancing.

Traditional African dance can be entertaining and enjoyable, but this is not always the sole intention. Many times, the dances are functional and as such can be considered "art for life's sake" as opposed to the concept of "art for art's sake." Traditional African dances are artistic and aesthetic and they are also utilitarian. Dances serve the society in furthering its goals, values, and ideals. Traditional dances are porous and reflect the influences of migration, intermarriages, religious changes, and technological advances. Often times, impromptu products like caps from soda bottles are used for musical instruments instead of the traditional metal that may typically be used. The sound is slightly different, but the convenience of recycling materials instead of having to hammer out the metal is worth it. This is how traditions gradually change. Dance, like other societal institutions, is a product of the times and reflects the times in which it exists. Belief systems change within the religion and outside of the religion, and again the dance reflects the change.

CIRCLE DANCES

Historically, the circle is one of the earliest spatial forms. When people lived in circular dwellings and enclosures, they danced circular dances. It was only after the progression to rectangular homes that linear and frontal dances were developed. The audience and spectator involvement in African dance is organized in a call-and-response format, which is complementary to the circle dance.

In dance, the circle may be large and open or small and tightly closed, with the dancers holding hands or linking arms. Large or small, the circle represents eternity and continuity. It is integrally connected to the idea of the perpetuation of generations and their progeny. All living creatures tend to move in nonlinear ways and everywhere in the world people have traditional dances that are circular. Snakes are generally perceived to represent the circle because of their ability to coil and connect their heads with their tails. In addition, it is widely believed throughout Africa that snakes have the ability to rejuvenate themselves.

This circular dance format, with choral audience oriented toward the drummers and surrounding and interacting with the leading dancers, remains, in fact, the dominant format throughout Africa—and in many other cultures around the world as well. The social implications of such a universal format are great and include call and response: an interaction between the singers, drummers, and/or dancers.

The term "circle-solo" dance captures two important qualities of African dance—the communal circle and the selected leader or solo. The circle represents a unified whole: The members of the group surrounding the central figure(s) are very close and involved in the dancing and with each other.

Unlike the linear format of Western performance halls, where the format distances each member of the audience from the others and from the onstage action, the audiences at performances of African dance are not separate observers but instead form a circular chorus. The fluidity of audiences in African dance is symbolic of a particular stance toward participation. Participation is anticipatory and responsive. In order for an event to be successful, everyone must be fully involved. Silence and stillness are not valued in the African performance arena. In fact, to be silent is to be critical in a negative way and to be still shows disdain and contempt for the performance. The music and dance should move the observers so that it is manifested in movements that include bobbing heads, shoulders shifting, hips rolling, and feet stomping or some variation of the theme. The social unification and interaction developed during these dances is the ideal or model for everyday activity as well. The emphasis placed on cycles and holistic unity in African society must be represented in the form of the dance that chooses to express itself.

The circle dance traditionally is inclusive of spectators and is the sum total of its performers and spectators. Even when African dance is performed on a Western stage, the dance accommodates the audience as the outer rim of the circle.

2

West African Dances

West Africa is rich with dancing and drumming traditions, and has given the world a panoply of dance traditions that continues to influence, inspire, and support artistic trends. This chapter is a sampling of representative dances from the region. Mask, rites-of-passage, healing, war, and funeral dances make up the larger portion of the dances listed in this chapter. Each of the following regions has dances that reflect the area's history, politics, and geographical climate. The climate of West Africa is tropical with a rainy and a dry season. The region is generally hot and humid with lush vegetation. The countries closer to the Sahara Desert have slightly different climates. Mali, Niger, Senegal, and Mauritania all have climates that reflect the dryness of being adjacent to the desert. Dances from Ghana, Nigeria, and Senegal are the most numerous in this text because scholars have done more research and documentation in these countries. Generally, more research has been done on West African dance because of the region's relatively close proximity to Europe and the United States. In addition, in recent years, many West Africans have come to study, work, and live in Europe and the United States, and have brought with them their cultural dances. These descriptions offer a glimpse into African culture and its dances. The role of dance in African culture is central to any study, understanding, and appreciation of Africa.

Dances in African cultures are multifunctional and they serve as a window into the ways in which many societies conduct and live their lives. West African dances run the gamut from stilt dances to funeral dances. Many of these dances pay homage to ancestors in some way. The dances that are described in the following pages are a small fraction of the dances that exist in the region. Documentation of the dances of Africa remains a challenge. While it is a given that dance is pervasive and integral to African cultures, it is seldom a priority to document because of more pressing issues such as poverty, health, and education. Consequently, the dances continue to be passed on traditionally until more documentation in the forms of videos, DVDs, and written text is available.

STILT DANCES

Stilt dances are dances that are performed on wooden stumps that elevate the dancer high into the air. Dancers strap wooden sticks onto their feet and lower legs, and they have the ability to dance and even jump on the stilts, delighting and engaging their communities. Stilt dances, like so many traditional dances in West Africa, are often mask dances. The dancer may be embodying a spirit or deity and needs to be masked for the occasion. During these times, the identity of the dancer is presumed unknown.

Chakaba are from Senegal, Gambia, Guinea, and the Ivory Coast, and use stilts that vary in height from five to ten feet.

Chakaba wears a headdress with side fringes and his body is clothed in African print costume that covers the body to the top of the stilts. The legs of the stilts are covered in the same material that covers the body. Some Chakaba wear a palm fiber or raffia skirt and carry a whisk, and many of the stilted figures jump rope.

In Benin, the Yoruba people do a stilt dance called Okparou and the Fon people perform Zangbeto. In Zangbeto, performers come out at night to ostensibly watch over the town. Villagers are aware of the Zangbeto but dare not come out at night lest they interfere with the security of the community that the Zangbeto has been entrusted to protect.

Gue Gblin is a stilt figure in the Ivory Coast who wears a black headdress with a plume of animal skin, topped with feathers that project from the headdress. The headdress has red side fringes and the face of the mask is black with a corded black tassel in the nose area. Gue Gblin wears a black-and-white-striped costume with matching pants that cover the legs of the stilts, and he carries a black whisk in each hand. The dance is very acrobatic and is accompanied by sets of triple-headed sangba drums.

MILITARY, WAR, AND MARTIAL ARTS DANCES

In West Africa, military, war, and martial arts dances are performed by men, but there are exceptions in some ethnic groups where women participate in or have their own war dances. In these dances, the dancers stylize their movements to depict war and conquest.

Korokoro is a Nigerian dance performed by men that consists of many kicks and arm thrusts, which are used to demonstrate how they meet opponents in war. Doundoumba is a Senegalese dance of strong men. Women do not traditionally perform movements from the Doundoumba, but when it is performed on stage, they dance movements from

The Ivory Coast is one of several countries in West Africa where the stilt dance is performed. The Chakaba, or stilt dancer, wears a headdress with side fringes and performs on stilts that range from five to ten feet in length.

the Mandiani dance. Instruments used include the djimbe, a goblet-shaped hand drum, which makes a high, crisp sound; and doun doun, doundoumba, sangba, and kenkeni—different names for different sizes of the same double-headed cylindrical drum.

Pele pele ka ngwu ji ana is the last dance of the Agaba performance. "Pele pele ka ngwu ji ana" means the little bird hops from one place to the other and is gone before people realize it. The masks and musicians exit the arena doing this dance. An Agaba performer must be strong and should have a high level of endurance because it is the nature of the mask to be perpetually on the move and be very aggressive. The Agaba mask symbolizes the physical strength and vitality of young men who kill animals in communal hunts. Thus the horns on the mask symbolize and dramatize masculine vigor.

The Women's War Dance is danced by the Ga women of Ghana whose husbands have gone off to battle. They mime the war experience through dance as an imitative charm. The women paint themselves white, adorn themselves with beads and charms, and carry guns, sticks, and knives. They hack paw-paw fruits as if they were enemies, carrying long brushes made of buffalo or horsetails as they dance. Another example is the Ashiabekor, a war dance of the Ewe people of Ghana, usually performed by war heroes to demonstrate the activities on the battlefield.

The Agbekor dance recounts the history of how the Ewe fought their way to the section of Ghana where they now live. It is a highly standardized dance and the drummer must change his patterns continuously because they are correlated to each element of the choreography. The dancers stylized their movements in keeping with the language of the drums and the situations of the war. The detail is fascinating in Agbekor in which the dancers move through a compendium of intricate rhythms, steps, gestures, and dance phrases.

RITES-OF-PASSAGE DANCES

The rites-of-passage dances or initiation dances often represent a child or adolescent's transition or even transformation into early man or womanhood. The dances range from detailed footwork all the way to a swing of the hips. The aesthetic qualities of the dances vary greatly from ethnic group and dances are often more than just figurative representations, often times they suggest an actual change in status or transformation from childhood to manhood or womanhood.

N'Goron is an initiation dance from the Ivory Coast for young women who are about to enter adulthood. This dance emphasizes vibrations of thoracic and abdominal muscle complexes. Rapid changes of rhythmic and step patterns from phrase to phrase, sometimes marked by punctuating pauses in the movement flow, characterize this dance.

Abang is a rites-of-passage dance where young women are shut away and "fattened"—spiritually and physically—and are subsequently displayed to the village chief and paraded before young and eligible men. The entrance of warriors and matriarchs accentuate this grand occasion. The chief wears a floral skirt, top hat, shades, and beads. His attendants carry his umbrella and fan. The young women are dressed in feathers, scarves, and shells. Some of the matriarchs carry gold shields and staffs; others balance immense headdresses of tinsel and multicolored pompons (flowers). Abang begins with the sound of drums. The chief enters surrounded by his umbrella and attendants, and as soon as he sits on his throne, a dozen young women enter in a line. First they move in unison, shaking their hips and beating intricate patterns into the floor. Then each woman makes a personal and often sensuous dance statement as if to prove that she is ready to face the world. With the entrance of the young women and the matriarchs, Abang becomes a visual spectacle. This processional ends with a communal burst of celebration that manifests itself in bold rhythms and complicated footwork.

Isiji encompasses all groups of Afikpo of the Ibo/Ibibio people of Nigeria. This dance celebrates the eldest son's initiation into the secret societies. Isiji is performed by young men, and they wear masks, a reddish-orange headpiece, and a light yellow raffia dress that stretches from the shoulders to the feet.

Domba is a Malinke word from Guinea. It was shortened from "Dembadon" meaning "happy mother." A mother performed this dance after the first night her daughter spent with her new husband. The mother of the bride would dance this dance celebrating the union of the two families.

Instruments used include the aforementioned djimbe and doun doun, doundoumba, sangba, or kenkeni.

Mandiani is a classical African dance that is performed all over West Africa and particularly in Mali, Guinea (where it originated), and Senegal. It is regularly performed in Europe and the United States and is in the repertory of major African dance companies in the West. Young girls perform Mandiani upon completion of their initiation and women performers often wear a short seurre decorated with pompons, cowrie shells, and pearls. These seurres can be cut in such a way that a variety of designs results when they are wrapped. Women may wear a headband or small hat. A cowrie shell-covered bra is also standard performance attire; or they may wear a belefete in combination with the cowrie bra. Men typically wear Arabic dress such as the grand bouba, turky, sabador, farug, thiayas, and dabas. Dancers and drummers often wear bracelets or amulets for protection. In community setting, all ages participate, including elders, and the basic movement does not vary for different dancers. Young people display greater variety and the tempo might accelerate for a younger dancer, but the basic movement remains the same for all ages. Songs used for Mandiani are ancient in origin but seldom retain the original text. The art of text improvisation is important and text can be changed to fit the occasion. There is not one specific song that is used for Mandiani everywhere it is performed, but one such song is an agricultural song that is sung in the call-and-response mode, which is used after a day's work in the fields or following the harvest. The basic posture for the Mandiani dance is with the knees bent and the upper body inclined forward at the waist (a forward pelvic tilt). The "triplet" is a rapid three-steps sequence seen in the Mandiani dance. Because of the speed and control required to execute this movement in Mandiani, the rhythmic subdivision can change based on tempo.

Another example of a rites-of-passage dance is the Satimbe, a celebration of the Awa society of the Dogon people of Mali, performed by one woman. She wears a beaded bodice or a bodice covered with cowrie shells, a grass skirt, bracelets, and a mask. The mask is a wood carving of a female. A chant is sung by the dancer and compares the female dancer to a stork.

The Gbongara is a graduation dance of the Senufo people of the Ivory Coast and is performed by children. The body is layered with raffia, feather headdress, and ornamental belts. Dangme girls are taught the Otofo dance, which is said to symbolize the utmost in femininity; its movements are designed to teach girls how a woman should walk and behave. The movements of the dance express feminine behavior: Simple and delicate foot patterns; the gentle thread of the feet on the ground; the deliberately controlled swing of the hips; and a calm, composed demeanor are all characteristics of the Otofo dance.

Finally, the Tokoe is a coming-of-age dance for girls. They wear scarves that are affixed to their index fingers. The dancers flick their wrists so the scarves move in accordance with the flicking action. The scarves are used throughout the dance; they are waved, furled, and unfurled. The significance is not the design in space or the color but the signal—which can be seen in the waving of the scarves—that alerts the community that the girl has come of age. The passing of the scarf through the palm shows that the scarf is being presented as proof of the coming of age.

MASK AND MASQUERADE DANCES

Mask dances are dances that utilize a mask and/or a full-body covering that conceals and hides the identity of the dancers so that the focus is on the figure. Mask dances can represent a figure or force from a secret society and secrecy becomes even more important on those occasions. As mentioned earlier, mask dancers often perform on stilts. The dancer performing the mask dance can wear a helmet-type headdress that also covers the face and these helmets can extend a couple of feet into the air. Cowrie shells, feathers, raffia, animal skins, and wood are some of the materials used for mask dances. Masquerade dances represent dances and songs that are known to the community and have a historical and ancestral lineage. The beauty and virtuosity in these dances reside in their distinct characteristics.

In Nigeria you will find the mask dance Ekine, which is also the name of the mask of the Igbo people of Nigeria that relates a story about Ekineba, a beautiful woman who was abducted by water spirits. Angry at what her children had done, the mother of the spirits told them to return Ekineba to her people. Before they did so, each of them showed her its special play, which she taught her people after returning home. When the people disobeyed the spirits' rule of beating the drum every time a play was put on, Ekineba was finally abducted for good. Ever since, she has been the patron goddess of the Ekine masking society. Before the plays, members pray for a good performance as well as for health, wealth, plentiful offspring, and peace. Dance is at the core of the Ekine plays.

Kakabotovi is a mask dance from Burkina Faso where the Kakabotovi figure comes out and mingles with the other performers. His purpose is to ward off and scare evil spirits. The Kakabotovi figure has a painted face as a disguise with body covering. Zaouli is a solo dance performed by a man in a young girl's mask and headdress. This dance is a tour de force of rhythmic virtuosity. An intriguing aspect of Zaouli is the rapid change of rhythmic and step patterns from phrase to phrase, which is sometimes marked by punctuating pauses in the movement flow.

There is a legend that states that around 1937, at the funeral of the oldest man in Nkpor (Nigeria), Nnunu Ozalla danced for the last time. Nnunu Ozalla is a miracle-making

Mask dances are performed throughout West Africa to ward off evil spirits. In addition to being danced during funeral ceremonies, the masked dance is performed during harvest ceremonies and is a right of passage for young men.

mask that performs feats because of its spiritual power. The mask danced until suddenly it began to circle. It then swept up to roof level, and imitated and actualized the ability of the bird to be airborne. A man dances the mask and his dress consists of a heavy raffia cover. The disguise-element in mask dances lends itself to mystical and magical powers because there is a degree of unknown that helps foster a belief in the powers of those things that are unseen or invisible.

Nwaotam is a mask dance designed to generate good feeling; people participate in the Nwaotam rite because it gives them physical, emotional, and psychological release. They are able to socialize with friends, and the dance is held in high regard because it is a tradition in Opobo (Nigeria). The dance ends with the mask jumping off a roof, which it is believed to have ascended to unaided.

Another mask dance is Ijele, which reflects the beauty, elegance, nobility, and wealth of the Ibo people of Nigeria. Ijele depicts Ibo life in all its complexities. Many animal, human, and spiritual figures are part of the mask. The mask is large (four to six feet high) and is sometimes considered the king of masks, although it can be subordinate to certain ancestral masks that are feared because of their mystical power. Ijele symbolizes the ingenious mind and the social solidarity of the people who made its construction possible. The mask dramatizes the high status and achievement of the ancestors. Cloth hangings sway in rhythmic response to the dancing of Ijele, the numerous symbols that hang from the headdress seem to tilt from side to side, the decorative mirrors glint in the sun, and the openwork headdress seems to revolve in the shifting scenes of color and design. While the mask is getting ready to come out, a woman named Nne Ijele (Ijele's mother) sings. During the mask's performance, there is a female chorus. The Ijele orchestra consists of drums, flutes, and a gong that plays "igba eze" (the music of kings) before the mask comes out. The orchestra also plays during the performance of Ijele. When the Ijele mask comes dancing out of the enclosure with slow, measured steps, it is preceded by a man and a number of escorts dance around it, invoking the spirit of the mask and guiding it along. As the mask seems to be possessed by the Ijele spirit, his burden begins to lighten and he goes into full motion. Ijele moves his massive body forward and backward, then from side to side. After dancing around the arena in his dignified manner, he goes into full motion, the new pace belying his monumental size. He then returns to the slow swaying again. Each movement of Ijele then becomes slow and majestic, enhancing his image as the king of masks and a figure of supreme mystical authority.

The mask Ekpe appears during the Ekpe festival, which was instituted in honor and thanksgiving to Ala, the Ibo Earth

Goddess. The climax of the festival is a sacrificial act by the Ekpe mask that reflects the struggle between good and evil. If it is successful, people believe there is moral victory of good over evil. Ekpe is a symbol of power, strength, pride, and heroism. Since failure of the sacrificial act spells disaster, the mask(er) prepares the dancer thoroughly for the act. He must rehearse his movements, perform his dance, and mime his sacrificial act. At the performance, when it is almost time for the sacrificial act, the tempo of the music increases until it is so fast that it seems no human being can dance it. But the mask does. After the quick execution of the act, the mask dances in celebration of the successful event. There are concentric circles of participants: the innermost (drummers and singers) who hold the mask; next a group of male performers; then women and young people; and finally guards. This is done to reinforce the masker. The dancers move slowly at first, gradually gathering speed. Their movements become more intricate, changing in rapid succession. Improvisation is widely used in African dances and in the Ekpe dance it is used to demonstrate and highlight the dancer's skills.

Ezembo is a mask dance/play in which an ancestral mask called Ezembo interacts with his wife, Ogoli, their teenage son, Akawo, and two young women in order to dramatize an exemplary family life. Ezembo is a model husband and father. Ogoli is a humble wife who respects her husband and sets an example for other women. She stands for the beauty of womanhood. Akawo stands for reckless- ness: he is troublesome and stubborn. Ada odo, one of the young women, is gentle, beautiful, and chaste. Ezembo wears a colorful dress—a combination of red, white, and yellow— and has ribbons and ornaments attached to his headpiece, which represent age and dignity. Ezembo carries a walking stick and a big, bright, colorful fan that is studded with small mirrors. As is the case with other female spirits,

Ogoli's mask is delicately cut and highly stylized. She has two projections in the form of breasts. Her costume is a tight-fitting velvet suit, made of the most expensive materials, e.g., Akwete (a woven cloth), and she wears expensive beads called aka. Akawo's costume reflects his reckless, stubborn character. He carries a machete, whips, or stick and stones with which he attacks the audience from time to time. Ada odo is made up like a maiden spirit, reflecting her gentle, beautiful character. No song accompanies Ogoli's dance for her husband, but she concludes the performance with a song in which she advises women to always respect their husband for that is wisdom.

Agaba or Agaba-idu is a Nigerian mask dance that literally means "lion." An Agaba performer must be strong and have a high level of endurance because it is the nature of the masks to be perpetually on the move and be very aggressive. The Agaba mask, which is two to six feet tall, symbolizes the physical strength and vitality of young men, who kill animals in communal hunts. An Agaba performer has a horned headdress, topped by crescent-shaped buffalo horns, and the narrow, pointed horns of various kinds of antelopes, which symbolize masculinity. Sometimes paddles and spears are added as hunting symbols of masculine strength or carved figures may be added. Agaba has a gaping mouth with several massive teeth showing. The traditional costume for Agaba is a two-piece suit of tough cloth covered with akwebilisi—large brown seeds that are attached in rows so they overlap and rattle. In modern times, the seeds have been replaced by bent pieces of metal, raffia, or small brass bells. The ogene men sing "Mmonwu anyi abia" (our mask has come) as the mask enters the arena. During the procession, two of the accompanying men play ogene (metal gongs) and before the masks enter the arena, two adolescent boys play ekwe (drum) and ofo. The musicians play and dance during the performance of the mask. Several sturdy men, who tread heavily and powerfully through the village, threatening spectators who stand at safe distances, accompany Agaba. Agaba's movements are irregular and erratic, and when taunted by the accompanists, Agaba shakes its rattling body furiously, stamping and rushing at spectators until attendants who hold a rope restrain him. In the arena, the mask, followed by elders, goes around greeting guests. Then the leader of the ogene men dances toward the mask and retreats. This symbolizes the relationship between the living and the dead (Agaba).

HARVEST DANCES

The earth is deeply respected and revered in Africa. This is particularly evident in the harvest dances where the performances express thankfulness for the fruits of the earth, a hunger that is of the past, and a purification of the ground and water. Often songs are used to accompany these dances in homage to farming and the earth.

Mendiane is a harvest dance that is sung in the Malinke language. The dancers perform intricate polyrhythmic footwork in which the legs stretch outwardly from the knee, as counterpoint to quick rotations of the wrist. The dance begins quietly in song and builds to a crescendo of exuberance.

Tyi Wara is an ancient homage to farming. The purpose is to invoke the blessing of the mystical creature Tyi Wara on the daily contest between the Bambana people of Mali and the stubborn soil. The Bambana people believe that they were put in contact with all the elements of the universe through agriculture. Men perform the dance and they wear a headdress with abstract, flowing lines in the shape of a man and animal. Women sing the Tyi Wara song, so that the men can become excellent farmers. Zou (Zouw) is a harvest dance of the Gio people of Northeastern Liberia. This dance is performed during the last week of the harvest season.

Odabra is an Idoma (Nigeria) word meaning "yams in abundance," and it is part of the "New Yam" festival. The dance steps express the hunger that the villagers have experienced and the joy for the sun and rain that has brought a bountiful harvest. Young boys 10 to 16 years old perform this dance.

Su, a fishing dance, commemorates annual fishing festivals. The dance has two parts: a ritual to clear the water and purify it for an abundant catch, and the actual movement of fishermen into the waters. Women who claim to be descended from fishing families perform Rawar Masunta or the fisherman's dance. Women hold a cloth in their hands, which represents the fishing net that is cast into the water. In order to cast the net successfully, a certain stance is developed which is mimicked in the dance. The body is carried in a forward high position and the hands imitate the collecting of fish. The hands are thrust into the water and slowly drawn to the waist, trapping the fish between the hands and the body as they are gathered.

Homowo is a corn harvest dance in Ghana. Special corn meal, called kpoi-kpoi, mixed with palm nut soup is prepared to celebrate the dance. Both men and women perform the dance and a special white cloth called the Caba is worn. Also from Ghana, the Sokodae is a dance to express thankfulness for the fruits of the earth, and it is performed by women and men. Kotou, from the Ivory Coast, is another harvest dance. It focuses on the yam harvest, which is a major source of revenue and sustenance for the people. Pairs of dancers carry long poles that they straddle, hoist, or balance on lifted thighs.

STORY AND MYTH DANCES

Story and myth dances tell the story of an important historical or current event, often with humor and a sense of awe. The purpose of the dances is to reenact a historical event; honor a deity figure or the heroic deeds of the deceased; and even to quell antisocial behavior. Singing is often performed. The song either serves as accompaniment to the story and myth dances or is performed as an actual part of the story. Storytelling is a powerful element that combines historical, educational, political, and social understandings.

Malissadio is based on a Guinean myth in which a beautiful village girl falls in love with Mali, the river god to whom she was promised at birth, and kills herself when the young hunter who desires her kills the hippopotamus-headed god. The Bell of Hamana is a story-dance from the Hamana area of Guinea. Like most good folk tales, it metaphorically tells the story of an important event with endearing humor and awe. A rough peasant woodcutter encounters a giant turtle, helplessly toppled over on its back. The woodcutter gently rights the turtle, which continues on its way with an amusing awkward agility. The woodcutter begins his work, but with each chop of his axe, the forest trembles with strange cries and lightning. Nature is offended and fantastic creatures, including a towering stilt walker, a roly-poly, and a hemp-skirted wood spirit set upon him in revenge for the destruction of their home. The turtle, master of the forest, saves the woodcutter and, to ceremoniously mark that moment, gives him a huge golden bell; the first bell of the Mandingo civilization of Guinea. The woodcutter takes it back to his gloomy village and it marks the arrival of a new, happier time for the village, which in turn begins a round of exuberant dances.

The Igunnuko dance comes from the Nupe people of Benin and is named after Igunnu, the deity associated with snare drum dances and the deity of fertility and good health who always brings rain, stops epidemics, and quells antisocial behavior. Igunnu is exceedingly tall, often reaching 12 feet or more, and has several graduated tiers of panels, streamers, or tassels in white color with red trim. Underneath the panels may be any multicolored and designed materials that are revealed when Igunnu moves and causes the panels to shift or wave. Near the bottom of the masquerade is a circular skirting of any color, which must widen when he expands his dance steps. A train may be attached, therefore covering the entire body. Singing is performed mostly by women but is taken up by men, whose songs usually differ. The song form is a short, often simple and syncopated drum beat. In addition, there are snared bembe drums, baabo ritual gourd rattles, with external strikers of cowrie shells, and dunkun (duku) pot drums. Among Igunnu's most notable characteristics are a sudden extension of height—and also an opposite and extreme lowering to the ground. Igunnu tilts, bends, widens, and contracts; twirls, swirls, bounces, stands upside down, and assumes numerous positions.

Nigeria's Nkwa Ese is a dance-play that takes place at an elder's burial and is a reenactment of the heroic deeds of the deceased. It is a reminder that his heroism could invoke the wrath of old individuals attending from other villages whose relatives had been his victims. This could lead to a serious battle instead of a mock battle. Sons and other male kin of the deceased dance the Nkwa Ese.

According to the late Ghanaian scholar, professor, and dancer, A.M. Opoku, the Bamaya dance of Ghana is about a man who was hungry and did not have money to buy food. Food is generally found where women are, so he decided to disguise himself as a woman to gain easy access to the market, where he stole a chicken. He was caught and unveiled. Men adorn themselves in skirts with frill around the waist to imitate the movement of a woman's hips in the Bamaya. There is usually a female singer who acts as the "crier" who alerted the authorities of the theft. This is one of the many examples of dances in which men dress like women in order to disguise themselves or mock women.

SOCIAL AND CEREMONIAL DANCES

Social and ceremonial dances are performed in both traditional and contemporary settings, such as a nightclub. The dances are performed to popular music, which often has political and ethnical themes. Various ceremonial dances—from ethnic group

Kwame Nkrumah (in suit), who served as Ghana's president from 1960 to 1966, his wife, and chieftains dance the Highlife, which is a West African social dance with political and ethical themes that is set to music.

to ethnic group—are performed by men and women at celebrations and festivals.

Highlife is a social dance performed all over West Africa but especially in major cities such as Accra, Ghana; Lagos, Nigeria; and Dakar, Senegal. It is danced for pure entertainment and performed in nightclubs. Highlife is not considered a cultural or traditional dance, but traditional people in villages perform it. Both women and men dance Highlife and the popular music that it is danced to often has political, social, and ethical themes. As a social dance, Highlife changes frequently and is often influenced by local, national, and international trends and events.

The Jobai dance figure performs in Sierra Leone and Liberia, and it looks like a huge mound of hay. The whole body is covered with liana (material similar to raffia) and resembles a haystack. The dancer wears a basket-woven pillbox cap atop his head. This hay figure can go completely flat and then regain its shape. It jumps and swirls around the dance floor and is exciting to watch. The figure can grow and diminish during performance.

The Takai dancers of Ghana carry an iron rod, and wear leather boots and a betekele ensemble (flowing robe and trousers with an elongated seat). The dancers perform a group dance in circles and strike their iron rods to create music. The dancers pivot and the robe and pants flow creating a design in space, similar to an umbrella that is opened and then twirled. The dance is percussively pulsated by the stamping of the feet and the striking together of the iron rods.

Zigribitz is a dance from the Ivory Coast that is performed by men and women. This dance features lightly performed hops, so light in texture it seems as if the dancers are floating on air. An intriguing aspect of the dance is the rapid change of rhythmic and step patterns from phrase to phrase, sometimes marked by punctuating pauses in the movement flow. Ibo women perform Itu nkwe as a coquettish walk-dance, which is a solo superimposition of impromptu, rhythmically free dance maneuvers over strict tempo rendition and group choreography. There are certain conventions that determine how far the soloist can go. The solo performer only interacts with those with whom she is closely acquainted. The dancers move slowly at first then gradually gather speed. Their movements become more intricate and confusing, changing in rapid succession.

Marpu is a dance of the Gio people of Liberia and its function is to entertain chiefs and special guests during the dry season (December–March). Marpu is performed by girls aged 10 to 14 and they wear skirts with bells around their waists. Igede is a Nigerian dance for celebrations, war, and funerals performed largely by men. Ange is performed at civic events now, but, traditionally, the dance was performed during marriages, funerals, and harvest celebrations. Both men and women dance it and they wear a fabric called Gberwar (hand-woven black-and-white cloth). Akya (flute) and the Gbagede and Agbande drums accompany the Ange dance. Totogiri is a Yoruba dance from the village of Western-Ipele in Owo district, Nigeria. The dance is performed at marriages and naming ceremonies. Asa/Agena is a dance that is performed by men for festivals and celebrations. They wear loose-fitting white gowns to allow for free movement of hands and legs. Gelede is a Yoruba dance from the western part of Nigeria and southeastern Benin. Gelede comes out when the village wants to select a new Oba (king), during significant ceremonies, or if an important person dies. The Gelede can be male or female and performs only at night.

Atsea (Achaya') is a secular dance of the people of West Togo and is performed by women. Dzimexe is a Togolese dance, which literally means "dance of the back" and is primarily danced by men at socials and funerals. Takai is a royal social dance in Nigeria performed by men who wear long leopard skin and feathers, and are accompanied by drums and hand-clapping. Bangumanga is a Ghanaian victory dance performed by the chief's children and wife for him at a ceremonial occasion, while Kpanlogo, also from Ghana, is a social, urban piece that was created in 1963.

FUNERAL DANCES

Funeral dances are performed throughout Africa, although some ethnic groups do not have dancing at burial rites. The dances that are performed signify the ethnicity, gender, and social status of the deceased. The dress that is worn encompasses a wide range of colors, textures, and ornamentation. In traditional African societies there were three groups of people who lived in every village. First there were those you could see—walking around, eating, sleeping, and working. Second were those waiting to be born and third were those who had passed on—the ancestors—to whom funeral dances pay homage.

Gona is a dance of the Dogon people that is performed at funerals and Dama ceremonies (special death anniversaries held every two to three years). The Dogon dances are ethnic dances but are performed more today as theatrical dances for tourists in Mali. This means a lot of traditional steps and movements have been left out in order to shorten the length of the dance. This dance is performed largely by a group of men known as the Society of Awe.

There are nine masks that are used in the dance, but the most common one is the Bede mask, which is made of black fibers and cowrie shells. Also used is the Sirige mask, which measures up to 20 feet and is made of the same material. Other accessories include dyed fibers that cover wrists, ankles, and the lower portion of the body. A drum, beating out the Oduboy rhythm, signifies the start of the dance, but there is a specific song that represents each of the nine masks.

Tyelige is a Kufulo and Fono people (Ivory Coast) funeral dance that is danced by young men who wear masks and a one-piece knit suit that covers the entire body. It is trimmed with multicolored raffia fringes at the waist and ankles. Yalimidyo is a funeral dance performed by graduate members of the Poro society of Liberia. Girnya is a Nigerian (Tiv) dance performed by men at the burial of an important man who has been victorious at war.

Fila and Kamuru are Senufo (Ivory Coast and Mali) funeral dances performed by male and female youths. In the Kamuru, performers wear a one-piece knit suit, belt of iron bells, and waist skirt of raffia. Gbon is a dance for funerals or initiations performed by men who wear high raffia polychrome collars that hide the base of a helmet-like mask. Layers of raffia wraps are attached to a full-bodied, dome-shaped mass of cream and crimson raffia. Koto is a Senufo funeral dance where the male and female performers wear a tight-fitting knit suit made of cotton cord yarn, black in color, with wrist and ankle attachments. Ewoh-ologba is a circle dance of the Egede society of Nigeria. Both men and women perform this funeral ceremony (idah). Traditionally men and women wore cloths wrapped around their bodies.

ANCIENT COURT DANCES

Court dances are often rooted in the precolonial era with both male and female African rulers. Adowa is a court dance from Ghana used for a variety of purposes. Elderly people dance Adowa to convey a particular message to the king in paying tribute and support. Princesses dance Adowa to pay tribute to the king and elders. The king dances Adowa to show his might and power when the drums beat a warlike tune. The battle cry of the elders can also be heard in this dance. The cry is fearful but an important aspect of the dance. If foreigners should be present, they are not allowed to participate in the dance. Traditional gestures are used to express thoughts and feelings of a funeral and both men and women dance the Adowa. Kente cloth is tied over the torsos of the dancers.

Iamgan is a classical dance with roots that go back to thirteenth-century Mali. Fouta is a dance that has evolved out of the old court dances of the royal house of Manding of Guinea. Kete is a traditional Ashanti court dance in Ghana performed by men and women.

WORK DANCES

Work dances figuratively suggest a man or woman carrying out various occupational tasks, such as the hammering of the blacksmith (Makera dance of the Housa people of West Africa), the action of meat sellers (Nama Hausa dance), or the work of fishermen casting nets (Ruwan Gwandon Kifi), and using spears and fish traps. Abofoo is a hunting dance performed both before and after the hunt. After the kill, the Abofoo dance is believed to purify the hunter of that special power that had been given to him for the specific purpose of enabling him to achieve his victory. Male dancers wear swirling, billowing capes to enhance their cat-like movements.

HEALING DANCES

Healing dances are performed to purify and clean an individual or community of people. Often the dances invoked an African deity who they identify as possessing the power to heal. Ekpo is a Nigerian dance performed by men and women and its purpose is to keep the town clean and to emphasize the good health of people. Tigari is a Ghanaian medicine dance performed to invoke a spirit of the same name.

The Bedu dance of the Ivory Coast is part of a purification ritual. The dancer visits every house in the village and blesses it. It is performed at the Bedu festival every year in December to bless and purify homes and their occupants from all evil in order to begin the New Year on a positive note. Males are entirely covered with raffia, made from tree bark, and they wear waist beads with a strip of cloth passed between the legs, headbands, leg bands called Bozani, and Bedu masks. Females wear two pieces of cloth called "Mammy cloth." The masks are carved from Onyina, a silk-cotton tree, and are painted in a variety of colors. Three drums control the rhythm of the Bedu dance: the Black drum is for males, the Tsulc drum is for females, and the Pinge drum is the supporting drum.

RELIGIOUS AND SPIRITUAL DANCES

Religious and spiritual dances are designated as those that are specifically performed to pay homage to a deity. Gahu is a religious dance of Togo and gives scope for individual expression and improvisation. Women perform it and they make music by rubbing together metal discs and bracelets. M'deup is a possession dance commonly performed by women. They make small shuffling steps and strong thrusts of their arms and head.

NATIONAL AND ETHNIC IDENTITY DANCES

National and ethnic dances are designated as those that show allegiance to one's national and ethnic background performed to songs that speak to national strength and loyalty. Kpegisu dance is closely linked to Ewe ethnic identity and is performed by men and women who dance in pairs or small groups. Okonkwo is a dance of the Ibo tribe that displays the skills of the best dancers in the community and is danced by men who wear wooden masks; decorated wooden or calabash caps and a red wooden headpiece; plastic waistbands and numerous small bits of colored cloth on the bodies and waists; and white shorts and ankle rattles. Atilogun is a dance performed to maintain cultural values and for ceremonious entertainment. Men and women perform it. Bands around the biceps and leg beads are worn and fresh palm is used to make skirts and ankle ornaments. Headbands are sewn to keep a large feather in place.

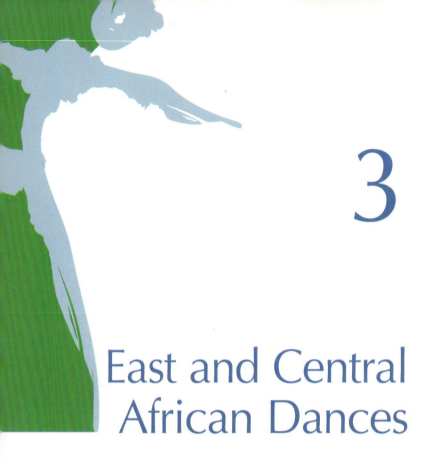

3

East and Central African Dances

East and Central Africa are home to many ethnic groups and thousands of cultures including the large Swahili ethnic group. East and Central Africa have some of the most beautiful flora and fauna in the world. Mt. Kilimanjaro, one of the world's tallest mountains, straddles the borders of Kenya and Tanzania. Some of the world's oldest churches are in Ethiopia, and Burundi and Rwanda are two ancient kingdoms nestled together in the Great Rift Valley. There are a large number of Muslim inhabitants in the region and Arabic has influenced the Swahili language and dance in East Africa.

HUNTING AND HARVEST DANCES

For many of the ethnic groups of East and Central Africa, hunting is a vital activity. In some cases, the food obtained from hunting is shared by the members of the community. However, hunting is not always fruitful due to a number of reasons:

Young girls of the Giriama ethnic group of coastal Kenya perform a dance in ringda skirts, which are made of nearly forty yards of white cloth.

amount of precipitation, deforestation, desertification, and exploitation of natural resources. Hunting dances are performed to ask the gods for good hunting when prey is scarce.

Molimo, performed by the Mbuti people of Congo, is sung and danced after someone's death, when hunting does not go well, or someone is ill. The men sing and dance the Molimo at night until the early morning and it can last as long as two months; but there is no set length. The dance may relate any of several legends about fire and Molimo. For instance, one story professes that women originally possessed the Molimo fire and that when an elderly woman stokes the fire, she symbolically gives it to the men to rebuild and revitalize with the dance of life. These legends bear witness to the importance given to fire by the Mbuti. In hunting groups, fire is essential to process food.

Younger men mainly participate in the Molimo, while the older men beat out a rhythm with *banja* sticks, and lead in songs of devotion and praise to the forest god. There are few words to most Molimo songs and most include verses that praise the forest because it is essential to the Mbuti's existance. While the men dance, the women and children are sequestered in their huts. No adult man is allowed to sleep while the Molimo is being sung.

Harvest dances serve as a way to thank earth for the bounty it has provided and to ask the gods for continued prosperity. An example is the Kilumi, which is a Kenyan music and dance type performed by adult men and women during drought season, when the god Ngai is asked to bring the rains. This seasonal music and dance performance marks "the ripening of the crops" and through it the Kamba people show their satisfaction with the fruits of the season. The harvest celebration includes the offering of the first harvested crops to the gods after which the people are free to eat the bounty. The original drum that was used to provide rhythmic accompaniment to Kilumi songs and dance was called *kithembe*. It was a cylindrical drum covered at one end (the top side) with goatskin known as Kithuma kya mbui, and was played with both hands when the drum was slanted and held between the knees.

Kilumi is also performed as therapy for those who are under the influence of a disease that is supposedly caused by the possession of demons (*akamba*) known as *aimo*. Kilumi is usually performed for the possessed to drive away the devils or demons that, at times, make the person have violent spells. Close relatives and friends accompany the possessed person in the dance and, in the process, some of these people are temporarily possessed by demons. The vigorous music making and dancing go on for many hours. When the rains are delayed, the old women, assisted by some men, gather to sing and pray to their god, and also to the spirits of the land whose favor or help they ask to bring down the rains. Kilumi songs may be used also as prayers to God to prevent disaster, to protect the crops from locusts and other pests, to drive away bad spirits from the community, and to assist rainmakers and medicine men in the foretelling of what is in store for people, whether good or bad.

Some East African people have songs and dances that are intended to stop the rain and save their crops. Ngutha is a very popular song that is danced to by young men and women between the beginning of the short rains and the early harvest. The drum sounds of Ngutha are believed to scare away the rains and, as such, this music is performed sometimes when the people do not want much rainfall. Dancers face each other in two lines, one for the men and the other for the women. The drummers form a third line. The women dance with the men they like or admire in the line. Boasting songs or short praise in the form of poems are sung when the selection of dancing partners takes place. The main aim for singing such songs/ poems is to attract the attention of the women. The main dance begins with the recitation of mwali poetry by the lead singer/dancer (ngui) who touches on themes like clan affairs, warfare, and wealth. Humorous songs for entertainment, as well as praise and insult songs, are also heard at the performances.

HEALING DANCES

In some places people believe not only in gods but also in spirits. Some of the events in daily life are explained as the result of the presence among humans of spirits of the dead or animal spirits. Illness, for instance, is seen as being caused by bad spirits that inhabit the bodies of the sick.

Ngoma/Mwase is a dance and music tradition performed by men and women in East Africa to help a "sick" person who is possessed and drive away the bad spirit that possesses the person. When a woman becomes possessed, she is taken to see a medicine man and, in most cases, the 'doctor' recommends the performance of Ngoma music and dance to the spirit. A little medicine or herbs are given to the patient by the 'doctor' after the music and dance performance, which renders the 'sick' person fit or restores her back to normal life.

The Ngoma dance, which is almost extinct, has been replaced these days with Mwase dance, which is similar in form and content to Ngoma. Kilumi dance drums were initially used to accompany Mwase music and dance, and the *kotola iito* shoulder rolling movement is employed in Mwase dance. The only musical instrument used today in Mwase is the *mukanda* drum.

INITIATION DANCES

As in other regions of the continent, dance in East Africa is part of rites and ceremonies that are celebrated to mark the passage of children or teenagers into new phases of their lives. Through initiation dances, these young members of the community are accepted as part of the group. Sometimes, initiation ceremonies prepare teenagers for adulthood, conferring them roles that require maturity, knowledge, and responsibility.

Nkumbi is an initiation dance performed by boys and older men of the Babira tribe of Congo. The children are separated from their families and taken out of town for several days. During this time, they only sustain contact with a group of older men who teach them songs and dances. When the boys return to the village, they sing and dance in public. *Makata* sticks are only used at the time of Nkumbi; each one is cut to a different length and tuned to a different pitch. The men tap a stick under their left arm with a shorter stick that is held in the right hand, and they dance around the village, playing a complicated but tuneful rhythm, the different notes overlapping and in combination.

Mingazi is performed by the Pende people of Congo and is danced after circumcisions. The dancers are clad in woven cloth, dried grasses, burlap, and animal skins, and are crowned with elaborate feathered headpieces. The dancers emphasize intricate polyrhythmic footwork in which the legs stretch outward from the knee as counterpoint to quick rotations of the wrists. Women are prohibited from viewing the dance.

The Pende of western Congo dance the Mingazi, a rite of passage performed after circumcisions. The dance emphasizes intricate polyrhythmic footwork and quick rotations of the wrist.

Men and boy initiates perform Authi music, songs, and dance when the boys have been circumcised. As part of the ritual, the boys stay at a circumcision camp for several days and receive instructions in martial arts and hunting. When the initiates are returning home from the camp after their wounds have healed they sing Authi songs. The Authi dance unfolds in a circular pattern that involves both men and circumcised boys. The men move in a circle while jumping and when they come down they all step forward once before low jumping only on the right leg. Inside the dance circle are two or three men who play a ruvaru, a carved flat piece of wood with jingles attached. The flat wooden board is beaten with a piece of carved stick (*ncuguma*) at one end to produce the rattling sound. These players also wear sets of ankle bells (*mikathi*) made of pellet bells tied together for dancing.

Sindimba is a puberty dance in Tanzania that shares some characteristics with both Mingazi and Authi. It is performed after successful completion of the rites of initiation, which are administered in seclusion in bush schools. Boys and girls dance the Sindimba and movements of the girls' hips are accentuated by a wrap of additional material tied around them. The boys wear looped fringes that hang from the waist of the shorts and play a vital part in shifting of the hips. The dance is accompanied by a host of musicians who play marimbas, rattles, and drums. Each of the drums is played with sticks with the exception of the *ntoyi* master drum, which is played by hand. In the Sindimba dance, emphasis is placed on the hips. The master drummer puts the dancers through a series of different movements, always returning to the main movement: a subtle emphasis on the left hip that is initiated by the knee, while the torso is in a backward high position.

Nzaiko ya Ngingo is a circumcision dance performed in Kenya during the second initiation rite—the great circumcision called *nzaiko nene*. In this dance, two lines of boys and girls may be formed with a few drummers performing outside the two lines. The dance movements involve standing and nodding the head, and kneeling with the forearms bent at the elbows and swinging the arms. *Mikanda* drums are used to accompany this initiation dance and it is only in this dance that drums can be used during the circumcision period. Other dance groups may be invited to participate in the Nzaiko ya Ngingo dance.

Kamondo is an initiation dance into the Bwami Association, which is a form of government for the Lega people of Congo. Both males and females who participate in the Kamondo dance dress in hides, cloth, feather bunches, and masks. Aphorisms or forceful sayings accompany the dance as a way of reinforcing societal values and teachings.

COMPETITION AND RECREATIONAL DANCES

As can be seen in the examples of initiation, harvest, hunting, and healing dances, music and dance are often related to the celebration of rituals. However, there are many other dances whose purpose is mainly recreational. They are performed for the enjoyment of dancers and spectators during competitions, feasts, wedding, and other social gatherings.

The Geerewol perfectly illustrates how competition and entertainment are intertwined in dance. The Geerewol is both a dance and a festival that is performed by the Wodaabe people of Niger, Nigeria, Cameroon, and Chad at the end of the rainy season. The dance is the highlight of the year for the Wodaabe and more than a thousand people may camp in the same location during the dance. The application of makeup is the most important preparatory act for the dance. The makeup, red ocher mixed with fat, is the same for everyone, so that the dancers can be judged on the basis of beauty alone. Once the dancers' makeup is applied, each dancer puts on a woman's wrapper, pulling it snug around his hips and fastening it at the knees with a leather tie. This tie around his knees obliges him to take very short steps, which elongates his already long and narrow contour.

When the dancers are ready, an immense fire is lit and one of the elders advances to invite the dancers to begin the dance. Only the most beautiful—about 50—dare to participate. They approach the fire in little groups, taking the short steps necessitated because their knees are bound. They position themselves in a long line, shoulder to shoulder. Without moving at first, they begin to intone a chant unique to their lineage.

The chant continues as the dance itself begins. On the beat, the 50 or so dancers, standing elbow to elbow in one line, rise to the tips of their toes, slightly bending their knees, and swing their arms forward in a long, elegant motion. At the same time, they turn their heads alternately to the right and left, their broad, almost theatrical, smiles showing off the whiteness of

A wedding dance is performed in southern Sudan.

their teeth, and they open their eyes very wide. As they dance, they tirelessly repeat the same refrain. They then fall silent, and others who stand in a row behind them answer in chorus. The chant ceases and the dance changes beat dramatically. The dancers advance in short, rapid hops. The metallic sounds of the ornaments on their ankles strike out, depending on the movements of their feet, an alternation of strong and weaker beats. Low, dull thuds resound as they stamp the ground with the flats of their feet, at the same time brandishing and twirling their ceremonial staffs. Then, making a quarter turn to the south, still taking short, jumping steps, they form a long single-file line that stretches for several yards. With another quarter-turn, to the same beat, the dancers return to their point of departure and realign themselves.

After several hours of uninterrupted dancing, three of the most beautiful women (surbaabe) are selected. The three chosen surbaabe slip off their sandals and move in a single-file line into the semicircle of dancers. They advance very slowly, their left hands held beside their faces and their eyes demurely lowered. They are then placed in line facing the dancers. After about 20 minutes the surbaabe rise, and each one—gracefully swinging her right arm and with her left hand still held against her left cheek—walks slowly toward the dancer she finds most beautiful and captivating. She almost touches him and then draws away while the audience shouts enthusiastically. Her choice has been made and thus the dance concludes.

In addition to the Geerewol, the Ruume, a circular dance with songs and clapping, and the Yaake, a dance in which dancers try to outdo one another through their facial expressions, are dances performed during the Geerewol festival.

The Yaake dance is performed with the participants in a line, shoulder to shoulder as in the Geerewol. The spectators position themselves in a semicircle facing the dancers, men on one side and women on the other. The dancers move slowly forward, alternately bending the knees and rising on tiptoe, while nodding the head in time with the beat. In this dance, the emphasis is on facial expressions and differs from one dancer to the next, but all have the same purpose: to bring out the whiteness of the eyes and of the teeth. The dancers wag their heads and roll their eyes or open them so wide that their eyes cross. They open their mouth and smile, then close and immediately reopen them, making their lips quiver. They also click their tongues and make kissing sounds. These noises are interspersed with the shrill, encouraging cries of the spectators.

Not all competition dances are about beauty. In some cases, dance in and of itself is the criterion to choose the winner. Mwasha is a women's dance of Bajuni origin, which was introduced to the Malindi district of Kenya from Witu in 1913. The dance is held indoors, and it is by invitation only. No men are allowed to be present, except those who are in the orchestra. It is often danced in competition with another dance group. The orchestra consists of a *vumi* (drum), *tari* (tambourine), and a *zumari* (clarinet) played by men. The competitors line up in two or three rows, one behind the other, and move forward slowly, an inch or two at each step, while they thrust their chins forward and move their shoulders in time to the drums. When the front row gets up to the wall of the room, or to the limits of the dance floor, all dancers face about and move slowly as before in the opposite direction, the front row becoming the back one. This dance may be derived from the Somalis and is very exciting to watch and perform.

Additional recreational dances are related to children's games, adult social gatherings, or for giving thanks after the harvest. Mukanda is an example of a thanksgiving dance that is performed in Kenya by girls and boys between April and June to give thanks for a good harvest. Mukanda is known in other Kamba areas as Mbeni. This music/dance type has borrowed steps and musical features from other dances of the area and came into being after World War I.

Older girls and circumcised boys perform Ncungo for recreation after the harvest season and before the rains come. Three or four *ngutha* drums are used to provide music accompaniment to this dance. A double and/or single flute/pipe called *mbibi* also provides music for the dance. The drums are beaten to call people for the dance at an arena specifically prepared for the performance. At the dance arena, girls select the boy they want to dance with. Couples stand facing each other before the dancing begins. The girls put their hands on the boys' shoulders and the boys in turn hold the girls' waists. They then start the dance by going down and bending their knees, and getting up while straightening them. All of the dancers move down and up at the same time while holding on to each other. The dance goes on until the singing and drumming cease. The Kigwa gwi song ends the Ncungo dance performance. The singing and dancing usually takes place in the girls' homes and songs performed or sung are not only those of Ncungo but also from the repertoire of Kinnguri and Muturu. Singing, drumming, and dancing take place from house to house at night during the dry season.

Another Kenyan entertainment dance that is performed by young boys and girls is the Nzai/Kiole. An interesting feature to this dance is that boys and girls blow a whistle during the performance. Nzai begins with solo songs after which singing takes place, accompanied by slow but steady dance movements. The third phase of singing in this dance performance is done in a strict rhythm and faster tempo.

Children aren't the only ones who perform entertainment dances. The Oaoi is recreational music and dance that is performed by men and women. The acrobatic dance is very energetic and it gives each performer an opportunity to show his or her skills. Oaoi dance movements differ from one another and they are performed in sequence accompanied by songs and dynamic and rhythmic drum music.

Although many recreational dances are tied to nature, others such as Tanzania's Beni dance originated in urban areas. The Beni was a response to British colonization and provided a sense of oneness for the people of Tanzania. In times of war and peace, it was a status maker, supplying the people an outlet to display their modernity and standing in society. Beni is an indigenous dance form created to display self-respect and self-confidence in communal values and express group pride based on locality, ethnicity, and/or class.

The Chama may be called a competition dance, owing to the element of rivalry that enters into it in regard to some other group that has also organized a dance. The men do their best to make as fine and big a show as possible in order to eclipse the dance of the competition. The dance used to be accompanied by a feast. Rival feelings sometimes run high, and if two competing dances happen to be taking place on the same night, it is not unheard of for one party to attack the other with sticks.

The men dress up in their best clothes and wear Arab daggers and swords borrowed from their friends. The orchestra consists of a vumi drum, a chapuo drum, a pair of vitasas, a zumari, and a tari, which is sometimes ornamented with loose brass discs that jingle together as in the Spanish tambourine. Goatskin is pegged to the wooden frame and is tightened by stuffing a thick cord between the skin and frame. The dance itself resembles the Arab Razha dance (see chapter four): the men standing in a row and twisting sticks in the same manner that the Arabs twist their swords, one of which may sometimes be seen in the hand of a Swahili dancer during the Chama dance.

Kinanda is a dance performed for the amusement of onlookers and is held indoors. It is considered risqué in conservative quarters of the community. Sometimes, the dancing is dispensed with and the entertainment is reduced to solo songs accompanied by the *kinanda*. It then assumes a more respectable character, though still not entirely approved of by religious groups. The musical instruments consist of the small marwasi drum and a kinanda, which supplies the tune. The latter is a stringed instrument of the nature of a guitar and is played in much the same way. It usually has seven strings, six of which formerly used to be made of sheep gut but are now made of twisted silk. The seventh is the bass string and is made of copper wire. While executing various steps and figures, two male performers hold a silk scarf or woolen shawl between them and repeatedly advance toward the audience and retire. They then face the audience and dance in that position, executing with their arms and bodies slow and graceful movements.

Dandaro is rarely danced by the upper classes and may be performed during the daytime as well as at night by both men and women. Occasionally, food may be cooked and partaken of toward the end of the dance. In the larger townships, no invitation is necessary and anybody may join in. A zumari plays the tune to which the dancers perform.

Mwaribe is a women's dance that is often performed at weddings, when betel nuts and cigarettes are handed around with tea. Toward the end of the entertainment, meat and rice are eaten. It may also be danced on the occasion of other celebrations like the first week of the northeast monsoon, in November and December. One of the women sings a solo, while the rest of the women sing the chorus. They clap their hands in time to a triangle. No drums are used. The women stand in a circle singing songs and clapping their hands. One dancer then advances, executing various movements, and then she retreats and another dancer comes out.

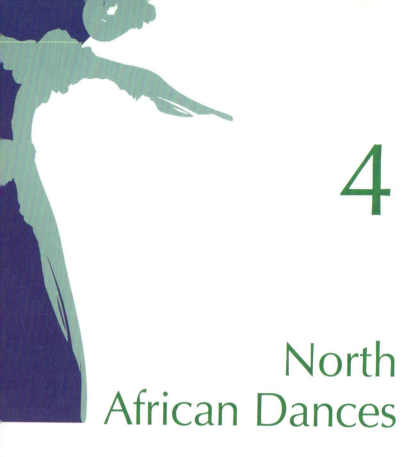

4

North African Dances

ANCIENT BEGINNINGS

The Tassili N'Ajjer Mountains are in Algeria, near the Sahara Desert in North Africa. At one time this region was moist and largely inhabited. There are about 30,000 cave paintings and engravings in the region, the earliest of which date to around 4800 B.C. Mask dancers can be found in some of the paintings, leading researchers to believe that the people of the Sahara influenced both Egypt and western Africa, both of which are known for using masks in their dances. However, the style of the Saharan masks is different from that of West Africa.

Dance and music held great importance in ancient Egyptian society. Laborers would work in rhythm, encouraged by the voices of workers and by the sound of their tools striking the earth. As civilizations were being molded into the complex web of societies that we know today, Egypt was in an advanced state and incorporated dance into every level of its society.

Dancing in public was an activity for the masses. The upper echelon of society could hire professional dance troupes for entertainment, and wealthy and noble Egyptians often had slaves trained to dance for special occasions as well. In addition, women from wealthy harems were trained in music and dance. However, the more responsibility a woman had in society, the less she would dance, even in private. Although dance was highly regarded and appreciated, it was strictly seen as a lower-class activity.

There were several occasions during which dance played a large role. Such occasions included both religious and nonreligious festivals, banquets, combat dances, and street dances. A widely celebrated religious festival was that of the god *Bes*. The priests of the town would hold a celebration for Bes, which was a solemn, processional ceremony with statues. After this ceremony was complete, the citizens of the town held their own celebration. On the day of Bes, no work would be done on the pyramids. There would be a parade through the town in which the participants would wear masks in the likeness of Bes. Dancers and tambourine players would march and children would run with them, clapping in rhythm. The villagers would join in singing from rooftops as the parade passed by.

Harems played an important role in the preservation of dance and music. In harems, women would learn dance from a dance mistress and also learn to play several instruments, including the lute, harp, lyre, and religious instruments such as the *sistra* and *mentis*. Dance in harems was more developed as a result of the women's isolation and their devotion to dance and music. Harems incorporated elements such as solos, pas de deux, pas de trois, group dancing, pyramid-like acrobatics, and, most importantly, set choreography.

Two dancers ca. 2400 B.C. Egyptians incorporated dance into every level of society, but despite the nobility's appreciation for it, dancing was largely a lower-class endeavor.

An example of the importance, respect, and legitimacy that dancers enjoyed can be seen in a letter that was written to a woman named Isadora, requesting her services at a party. It can be inferred that Isadora was a free woman, not a slave, because she negotiated her own contracts. The traditional name for an Egyptian dancer was *orchestria*; Isadora, however, was a *krotalistria*, meaning she specialized in dancing with castanets. She was hired for a specific date, at a specific location, and her employer provided transportation for Isadora, her dancers, and her props. Her pay was outstanding. A typical bricklayer of ancient Egypt received about 2.5 drachmas per day; a skilled weaver about 7.5. Isadora, however, received a startling 36 drachmas per day, showing the high regard for trained dancers.

Movements that today would be considered both pedestrian and classical were incorporated into Egyptian dance. Traveling steps such as fast and slow walking, stamping, running, short hops, and leaps were used. Body posture was free, allowing the dancer to lean forward, back, and to the side, while incorporating hip, belt, shoulder, and waist circulation. The spine could either be stiff or relaxed. This freedom of the body is what largely separates ancient Egyptian dance from its successor, belly dance. Dancers could either speed or retard their movements, following preference or the music. Whole- and half-turns were used. The hands were traditionally relaxed; however, fists and rigid palms could also be incorporated. Tools such as castanets made from wood, bone, or ivory; short curved rattle sticks with heads of gazelles; and canes and finger cymbals were frequently used in the dance.

Egypt was a large and advanced power that began to branch out and accept foreign influences. About 1500 B.C., Bayaderes, temple dancers from India, came to Egypt. They moved in soft lines—never moving sharply or bending—and influenced the Egyptian styles.

The Medieval period brought about a new form of dancers called the Ghawazee, which literally means "invaders of the heart." They were gypsies who resided mostly along the southern Nile and in Cairo, and were terrorized and killed by the French ruler Napoleon Bonaparte and his generals in the early 1800s. Napoleon never saw the Ghawazee dance during his invasions because the Ghawazee refused to allow the French to view their culture. When Napoleon came to their city, the gypsies left, only to return when Napoleon was gone.

Ghawazee costumes changed in response to foreign influences, mostly by that of Turkish and Persian styles. Dancers wore fitted tunics, replicating the fashion from the women in the courts of the Ottoman Empire. They wore low-cut bodices; large, full skirts; bulky hip-scarves; three-quarter sleeves with scarf-like, excess fabric hanging from the sleeves that was influenced by new Persian coats; fitted jackets; sheer blouses; small, fitted vests; and low-slung, flowing skirts or Turkish-style "harem" pants.

Men often performed a cane or stick dance known as Tahtib. The men would use a thick, solid bamboo staff called an *asa* or *asaya*, or a *shoum* or *nabboot*. This staff was often carried on long journeys, especially at night. The Tahtib dance is the oldest form of Egyptian martial art that has survived. This dance is usually performed at weddings, welcoming parties, or harvest festivals. Not only was it practiced as an art form and recreational activity, but it was also a form of self-defense.

Ancient Egypt was a nation rich in culture, history, and innovation. The integration of dance into its society was important and the Egyptians' appreciation for dance and its development still continue to influence the dance world, as it laid the foundations for rhythm, movement, choreography, and style.

CONG BUL: RITES-OF-PASSAGE DANCE

Cong Bul is a dance from the Sudan performed by men. Although the Shilluk tribe had no elaborate and prolonged rites of passage for youths to acquire manhood status, participation in a Cong Bul dance for warriors and their partners was the measure of achieving adult status and a symbol of reintegration into the community after a brief period of separation.

SOCIAL AND CEREMONIAL DANCES

The Investiture dances of the Nubians in Egypt and the Sudan are religious and political dances performed upon the death of one *Reth* (king) and the ascension of another. The function of the elaborate rituals is not only to ensure the lawful succession to the throne but also to let it be known and seen that the essence of the people's heritage is properly transferred from the dead monarch to the body and soul of the king-elect.

All able-bodied Nubians participate in the Investiture dances. By joining in, they become part of the process of bestowing the stamp of legitimacy on the new Reth. When alive, the Reth embodies the dual spirit of *Nyikang* (the collective ongoing existence of ancestors as well as the power of a higher, supernatural force).

When the king dies and a new king-elect is enthroned, a special dance is performed. The "army" of the king-elect meets the "army" of Nyikang. The army of the king-elect is defeated and he is captured by Nyikang and taken to the capital. The "battle" of the armies is in effect a stylized group dance. The "spears" are millet stalks. The action of attack is simulated, as is defense. The high point is the capture of the king and the moments of trance that ensue. Another mock battle follows in which the king is rescued. The king then marries a girl and after the king's enthronement, Nyikang seizes the girl and refuses to surrender her to the king. In the mock battle, the king's army is victorious and he takes back his wife. This mock battle transforms the king's status from underdog to victor.

Ngoma ya Fimbo, or walking stick dance, is a celebratory dance performed by men at wedding feasts and circumcision feasts. The dancers carry walking sticks and assemble to form a ring in the open near the house of the host. While those in the ring balance themselves slowly and rhythmically from one foot to the other, two of their number go into the center and make passes at each other with their sticks as if they were swords. Cigarettes and betel nuts are passed around to the dancers. Vumi, a large bass drum (2 to 3 feet long and 15 inches in diameter), and *chapuo* drums (18 inches long by 8 in diameter), which are cylindrical in shape and covered with goatskin on both ends, are played during the performance along with brass *vitasa* cymbals, and a zumari clarinet. In a temporary pavilion of palm-thatch erected close by, a number of young women hold buffalo horns in their left hands, which they strike with small sticks in time to the drumming.

Shebwani is another dance performed at weddings. Arab men of Mkelle or Makulla perform the dance without any weapons and they attend by invitation only. The dancers sing a chorus song and keep time by clapping their hands. The orchestra consists of a vumi and chapuo drum, which is played on both ends with the hands, while hung across the waist of the drummer by a cord around the neck. The vumi is beaten in the same manner as the chapuo. A treble drum called *marwasi* is also used. It is much smaller than the vumi: only about 8 inches long by 8 inches in diameter. It is covered with goatskin on both ends and is beaten with the flat of the right hand, while held in the left with a piece of cord. Vitasas are also used to accompany the drumming.

The dance of the Bou Saada is from Tunisia and is danced by women. They sing in couplets alternately in Sudanese dialect and wear costumes that have multicolored paper crowns and skirts made up of reeds, feathers, and shells.

The Dance of Stambali is a specialty of the Tunisian Negro Brotherhood Arifa. They cover their hands with red handkerchiefs and then their feet strike the ground in cadence, while their shoulders make a movement as if throwing off a heavy load.

Hatharmut men dance the Sherha in commemoration of a wedding or other celebration. The music is supplied by a zumari, which is accompanied by a vumi drum and a large high-toned *msondo* drum. The dancers stand in a large circle some ten paces in diameter and sway their bodies slightly from side to side, while clapping their hands in time to the music. Presently, two men come out of the ring and dance toward each other, and then backwards and forwards in a sort of mock chase for about ten minutes. Then they leave the ring and are replaced by two others. Sometimes two couples dance in the ring at the same time.

Vugo is a wedding dance where a procession of women is often formed in the evening after dark to parade through the streets. The women sing in chorus to the sound of buffalo horns that are beaten with short sticks.

The Zamil is danced in front of the house of the person in whose honor it is held, either by day or night. It is not by invitation and anyone may join in. The leader of the dance starts singing a solo, usually a song of praise to the honoree, and the remainder take up the chorus, which is accompanied by rhythmic clapping of the hands and swaying of the body.

Gogo is a women's dance of rebellion, consisting of socially approved cross-dressing behavior on the part of women, which is believed to be for the common good. When the Gogo men, who hold ritual responsibility for human and livestock fertility, fail in their duties, disorder reigns, and women assume the men's ritual roles and become the only active agents permitted to redress wrong.

Shangwi is identical to the Chama and is danced by the winning faction in the Chama competition, which is judged by the "wazee wa Ngoma" or elders of the dance: men who are the masters of ceremony. The winning faction proceeds to the house of the organizer of the opposition dance and they dance the Shangwi in front of it. The head of the opposition is supposed to take this as a compliment, and passes around a scent bottle, while sometimes taking part in the dancing himself. The Shangwi has no mystical meaning and is usually performed at night. The orchestra consists of a vumi drum, a chapuo drum, a pair of vitasas, a zumari, and a tari. The men stand in a row and jerk their swords, one of which may sometimes be seen in the hand of a Swahili dancer of the Chama.

WHIRLING DERVISH

Whirling Dervishes, known as the Mevlevi Order of Sufi Muslims, practice a devotional dance called the Ritual of Sema in Libya, Sudan, Egypt, Tunis, and Morocco. Dancers tilt their heads to the right and stretch out their arms as they spin round and round in a precise rhythm in order to achieve a trance state. The ceremony, which can last for hours, represents a spiritual journey; the dancers turn toward God in hope of establishing a greater understanding and union with God. The dancers wear a white skirt-like garment that billows as they turn.

BALADI (BELLY DANCE)

Although there are several names for belly dancing in Egypt, Baladi is most commonly used. The Baladi is performed at weddings, birthdays, parties, and public festivals such as the Mawalid or Saints' Days. It is also performed in clubs, hotels, and theaters and is usually part of a larger program of entertainment. There is often a singer and almost always live musicians, including a drummer. Wedding songs are sung and the drummer plays the special wedding beat (zaffat al arousal). A drum is always played and at weddings there are both drummers and a flutist. The lead drummer controls the dance and good musicians help train the dancer

Whirling Dervishes participate in the Ritual of Sema, a religious ceremony in which dancers enter a trance-like state in order to receive the energy of God. In Africa, the dance is practiced in Egypt, Libya, Morocco, Sudan, and Tunis.

and improve her dancing. Classic instruments used in addition to the drum are the *ud* (lute), *nai* (flute), and *mazmar* (oboe-type woodwind). In a way, the dancer is a musician, using her body to express the music.

Audience participation is also important. During a wedding, the band and dancers perform during the procession of the bride and groom to the hall of festivity. Because the focus is on the bride and not the dancer, the dancer performs a simpler version of the belly dance. The dancer may perform again later on, which may also include a singer of Egyptian songs and a band playing foreign music. If the dancer's second performance is the final part of the wedding, she will dance the newlywed couple out the door. The Baladi has few movements but may include "snake hands" undulations, "side hips" shimmering, the "hip roll," chest movements, and chest and shoulder shimmies. The dance is mainly performed as entertainment. Baladi is loved but not esteemed, because it is not performed by the upper class. Many women who dance Baladi do so as a way to escape poor circumstances. The Baladi is not sexual and the movements are not looked on as sexy. Yet the belly dancer carries a stigma that she is using her body to make a living and thus is immoral. In small poor cabarets, the dance is sometimes associated with prostitution. The dancers are usually of lower social class because to them economic gain outweighs social disapproval. While they grow up, most girls learn to dance by watching others. However, retired dancers often set up schools to train others. This stress on class and education may go back to an old Egyptian tradition of a need for a dancer to be an *alma*, or a woman of learning.

As entertainment, the Baladi can have a therapeutic effect: the dancer brings joy, happiness, and cheerfulness to those who watch; she helps bad moods vanish. During a show, the dancer may wear two different costumes, which show off the torso and midriff areas in particular. The ideal costume is reserved but elegant and fashionable. It should be expensive, with elaborate detail demonstrating its value. The belt is usually beaded with long, swinging fringes; shows off the hips, and through the hips, the dance. The color of the costume should be bright and dramatic, and should complement the dancer's body. A veil is often part of the outfit. A skirt with many layers is preferred, as it will move beautifully through-out the dance. Most dancers perform in bare feet. Sometimes a cane, which is balanced on the chest and belly, is used in a dance performance. Other accessories include *sagaat*, small cymbals attached to the fingers. Women are the main performers of Baladi, although men have danced the Baladi and sometimes still do.

In general, a dancer should perform for a long time. Audiences really appreciate the execution of a long and difficult movement, repetition of the same movements, utilization of intricate hand movements, good musicians, and décor and atmosphere. Dance skills involve virtuosity, creative use of elements of the dance, and fully developed personal dance style. The dancer must be "mature" and express herself and her experience through her dance. Egyptian women in general are said to have a special grace that manifests itself distinctively as they move. Walking and dancing are closely linked and the Baladi is a very body-oriented dance; if one cannot see the muscles move, one cannot see the dance. Muscle control is essential to good dancing and a dancer has to be able to move each muscle separately. This skill is especially evident in the slow part of the dance. Also important is continuous movement of the body from the waist down. All in all, the movements of the body have to be in harmony and balance; one part should not distract from the overall movement of the body. Body flexibility is critical. The dancer has to be able to move softly without effort, like a fish in water. The waist should be like a hinge: a joint between top and lower body. The dancer's face should be lively, charming, and relaxed, not provocative.

There are contrasting opinions on the origins of the Baladi: some say it originates from Turkey, with elements of Egyptian dance fused into it, others hold that it is an ancient Egyptian dance with Turkish (Ottoman) influences. Recently, belly dancing has had two major obstacles to overcome. During World War II, European troops demanded that belly dancing be performed as entertainment at nightclubs, which lowered its standards. More recently, the dance has been under censorship attack from the Muslim government, which has issued laws prohibiting certain motions and requiring belly dancers to cover up their bosom and belly.

ZAR HEALING DANCE

In Egyptian Nubia, the main purpose of a *Zar* ceremony is to cure emotional or physical disorders, through contact with the possessing spirits believed to cause such maladies. Though Nubians possess several methods for dealing with psychological disturbances, the Zar is a last resort, one that has powerful therapeutic effects for several kinds of ailments. The Nubian Zar ceremony is essentially a means of dealing with the demonic powers of evil, variously called *gour* (Mahas Nubian), *shantan afrit, iblis, jinn* (Arabic), or Zar spirits, who may cause illness. The whole direction of the ceremony is toward propitiation and persuasion of a spirit-being rather than coercion of them. Before trying Zar, most patients have already been to diviners or healers such as the sheikhs of the hajab (charm makers), who use the Qur'an (Muslim holy book) to exorcise jinn. Zar ceremonies vary considerably in detail according to the idiosyncrasies of the practitioner of "Sheikh of the Zar" and the type of illness being treated. Although some Zars focus heavily on social, entertainment, and divination activities, their major concern is with treating mental illness and certain features are common to most ceremonies.

When a Zar is requested, the sheikh (male) or sheikha (female) begins by asking questions about the patient. The Zar is primarily a female activity, though males often play the principal roles of leader and musicians, and the core of the typical Zar audience is composed of women who regard themselves as having been helped or cured. Anyone may attend the Zar, but it is felt that men should not attend women's ceremonies and vice versa. The setting of the Zar is usually a house with a very large room, because the audience numbers from 30 to 100 or more. A cleared "stage" area in the center is needed for the sheikh and his/her helpers, with enough room for the dancers. It is important to keep the room filled with the fragrance of incense and perfume, and a censer (covered incense burner) is passed around the audience several times during the performance.

On entering the room, each woman leaves her shoes at the threshold and places five or ten pilasters on the sheikh's tambourine. All those attending the Zar wear new or clean clothing to please the "masters," as the inhabiting spirits are sometimes called. The main patient usually wears a white gown, *jalabeya*, and a white veil, *tarha*. Her hands and body are dyed with henna, and her eyelids are blackened with kohl. She also wears as much gold jewelry as possible, is heavily perfumed, and sits like a bride, looking straight ahead. If the patient is a man, he also is adorned as a bride.

The sheikha begins the ceremony proper with songs and drumming. The form of the songs adheres to a typical Nubian pattern of verse and refrain. The dance is very postural. The use of effort is even, except for some emphatic movements such as shoulder thrust and turns. She does not seem as rooted as the other dancers, because the shoes limit use of weight.

Female attendants (usually kin) help the sheikha change costumes in correspondence with the river creatures (demonic spirits) that possessed her in turn. The sheikha and some of the women sing. The possessed sheikha also talks in a forced falsetto, with the voice and manner of one of the river creatures, according to its sex and age. Some of the women beat tambourines. The performance begins in silence and the sheikha puts her hands on her knees, elbows outward, in deep concentration. The first signs of the oncoming trance are deep with extensive yawning that is interrupted by moments of silence and followed by her fixed stare. She then twists her arms and neck in a cramped and unnatural posture. Suddenly she jumps up, greeting the women with "Salamu aleykum, ya sittat!" (Peace be on you, women!), and while some women beat on a tambourine drum and sing, she also sings and simultaneously jumps up and down. All her movements are strong and powerful.

NGOMA YA PEPO (PEPO DANCES)

The Swahili word *pepo* is the equivalent of the Arab word jinn, meaning devil or evil spirit. Some evil spirits are harmless, while others, entering into the human body, create various ills and pains, insensibility, or sometimes a demented state accompanied by violent gestures. The majority of the people who get pepo are women. The native cure for pepo is drumming in honor of the evil spirit, which is supposed to put it in a good mood so as to induce it to depart from the body of the possessed person. A professional man or elderly woman known as *fundi* or *mganga*, who specializes in certain kinds of pepo, conducts the exorcising of the pepo. Pepo is classified as belonging to certain clans. The fundi interpret the speech of the possessed person, which they claim is an ancient form of Arabic, Somali, Swahili, etc. Each fundi has its own special set of pepo, whom he knows by name, and to him only will such pepo respond. If a fundi is unable to make the pepo speak to him through the lips of the patient, then he knows that the pepo is not one of his set, and he will suggest that another fundi be called in. The fundi administers *dawa*, an herbal medicine, to the patient to make the pepo speak so it can tell the fundi what it will accept as propitiation for leaving the body of the patient. The family has to pay a fee for the fundi and provide food for the fundi, drummers, and guests. The fee for the fundi is not paid until he has been successful in making the pepo depart. When a fundi has recognized a pepo as one of his own, he sends word to all the other fundis and invites them to witness his efforts to exorcise the pepo. Each pepo has its own ritual. The drumming and dancing invariably take place indoors until the last day, when the patient is practically cured and the dancing goes on outside the house.

New clothes must be worn for the pepo in all cases, and the patient must wear clothes that represent the pepo's clan. The patient's dress varies with different pepo rituals.

Pepo ya ki-arabu is one of several rituals for exorcising an evil spirit. The ceremonies, which are used to expel a pepo of this variety, constitute a type that is followed with slight variations in exorcising almost all the jinns believed to belong to Muslim peoples. The fundamental difference between the method of treating a traditional African pepo and Muslim pepo is in the substitution of strong perfumes for the Turkish bath method, in order to induce the pepo to declare himself. The ingredients used include rose water, ambergris, musk, saffron, and camphor. Using this as an ink, the fundi writes the name of Allah (God) on a plate with his favorite attributes as well as the names of some of the archangels. The writing complete, it is carefully and reverently washed off the plate into a cup and then given to the patient to drink. Incense is also burned beside him.

The patient wears new white cloths, and a pair of trousers, tight at the ankles, is also worn. A *maharuma* or bedouin headdress is secured on his head, but if none is available, an ordinary white cap will do. On standing up to dance, the patient must change his clothes. He discards his two white cloths, and if the pepo possessing him has been ascertained to be male, he dons a white kanzu (long-sleeved garment) as worn by men. If the pepo is female, then a short kanzu of colored material or, if possible, of silk, such as the Arab women of Muscat wear, is put on by the patient. During the dance, a small white flag is placed in each of the patient's hands, on which the verse of the Qur'an "ayal il kursi" is written.

He holds the flag in his left hand over his left shoulder and the flag in his right hand he waves about. Sometimes the patient rides a bull, and, if this takes place, he wears his best turban, a sword, and a dagger. Instruments that are used to praise the spirit include the vumi drum and the tari, which is sometimes ornamented with loose brass discs that jingle together.

The patient sits on a stool and gradually begins to sway his body in time to the music. Later on, the swaying becomes more and more accentuated, until it progresses into a state where jerks of the body of sufficient force move the stool on which the patient sits all around the room. Ultimately, he becomes sufficiently excited to stand up and dance with a sort of gliding step, moving backward and forward between the two lines of dancers who imitate his steps and gestures.

In the Pepo ya ki-galla, women are allowed in the sick room, along with the fundi, musicians, and one or two male guests. The patient is dressed in brand-new white cloths: one is tied around the chest for men or around the waist for women and hangs to the feet; the other is draped over the head and shoulders, leaving only the face visible. The dancing begins early in the morning and lasts for two or three hours, and the second session takes place the same day from about six to nine in the evening. This continues every day for seven days. On the third day, the pepo usually begins to participate in the dancing. While seated, the patient jerks his or her shoulders back and forth and up and down, in time to the drumming. Then he/she gradually rises from the seat. A fly switch made from the tail of an animal is placed in one hand and a small calabash (shell of a gourd used as a utensil) filled with leaves, which have medicinal properties, is placed in the other. A string of oval iron bells (*njuga*) is tied just below the right knee. The patient shuffles forward alone, feet dragging, takes up position between the two lines of dancers, one at each end of the room, and shuffles back and forth between them, while waving the fly switch and the calabash, and still jerking the shoulders in the same manner but remaining in the same place. This is repeated twice a day until the evening of the seventh day, when the dancing continues through the night well into the next day, sometimes even until midday.

Swahili is spoken by the fundi in the Pepo ya ki-ng'ombe but in a hesitating manner and interspersed with bovine noises. This pepo is said to make the patient moo like a cow and the pepo must be given grass. The patient is rubbed with castor oil, but no other greases or scents must be brought near him. As soon as the patient is strong enough, dark blue cotton cloths are put on him and he also wears a *shumburere* hat and a *torosi*, which is a leather breast and back plate connected by straps over the shoulders and profusely decorated with beads and cowrie shells. During the dancing, the patient carries a fly switch.

The patient first sits up and eventually takes part in the dancing. The dancers form a circle, one behind the other, and move around and around with short, jerky steps in a counter-clockwise direction and stamp their feet in time to the drums. They move the upper part of the body by alternately throwing the chest forward and the shoulders back and then the shoulders forward and chest in. The patient dances along with the others and waves a fly switch made from the tail of a mule or giraffe. The dancing may be protracted to three weeks, as the illness is sometimes very stubborn.

In the Pepo ya ki-rima, the patient wears a shumburere, which is exactly the same shape as a Mexican hat, with a tall, conical crown and a very wide brim. It is woven from the split fronds of the dom palm or the mkindu palm. From the outer edge of the brim is suspended a fringe composed of strips of colored cloth, which hang down to the pit of the stomach in front and to the same level at the back. The head and face of the patient are consequently hidden. There are some 40 songs of praise for the Pepo ya ki-rima. The dancers follow each other around and around, counter-clockwise. The patient waves a fly switch made out of the tail of a mule or giraffe, and is anointed with castor oil as soon as he/she shows signs of movement and indicates that he/she is about to begin to dance.

In the Pepo ya ki-sanye, the patient is dressed in two new dark blue cotton cloths, worn as a Swahili woman wears her leso. No headdress is worn. On the second day of the dance, if the patient is a woman, she exchanges her dark blue cloths for a kilt. The dance begins early in the morning and lasts about an hour and a half. The patient then goes about his work as usual. In the evening, the dancers reassemble and dance through the night with the patient. A line is formed, and one dancer at a time advances to where the drums are being played, jerks his shoulders about, while bending over one of the drums for a few minutes, then suddenly stamping his foot, he retires with a shuffling step back to his place in the line and another dancer comes forward and repeats the performance. The patient dances with the others but is distinguished by having a fly switch in one hand and a live fowl in the other, both of which he waves about. On the last day of the Pepo ya ki-sanye ritual, the patient dons a torosi and the dancers form a circle, one behind the other, and move around and around with short, jerky steps in a counter-clockwise direction, while stamping their feet in time to the drums. They move the upper part of the body by alternately throwing the chest forward with shoulders back and then they move the shoulders forward and keep the chest in. The patient dances along with the others and waves a fly switch made from the tail of a mule or giraffe. Like the Pepo ya ki-galla, this is repeated twice a day until the evening of the seventh day, when the dancing is prolonged through the night well into the next day, sometimes even until midday.

In the Pepo ya ki-pemba, the patient is dressed in brand-new white cloths; one piece is tied around the chest for men and around the waist for women and hangs to the feet, the other is draped over the head and shoulders, leaving only the face visible. On the eleventh day of the ritual, the patient carries a fly switch in his hand and has a string of oval iron bells tied to his right ankle. The patient wears no headdress but a paste made by pounding a scented wood called *udi* is applied all over the head. If no udi wood is available, the wood of the muhuhu tree is used. A half-inch-wide black line is also painted from the tip of the nose over the head to the back of the neck. The patient is placed on a stool, and as soon as the drumming begins, he sways his body about in time to the drum and ultimately jerks the stool on which he sits around the room. The jerking about on the stool goes on for seven days. On the eighth day, matting is laid on the floor. The patient sits on the matting at one end and proceeds to propel himself forward to the other end. On reaching the other end, he lunges backward without turning around. This is very laborious and takes a good deal of effort. On the eleventh day, the patient assumes an upright position and dances, standing up between two lines of dancers. He advances with short, shuffling steps to the line of dancers in front of him. On getting within a couple feet of them, he begins to leave, shuffling backwards without turning around and keeping his body bent forward almost at a right angle with his lower limbs. Both the line of dancers who face him and follow him keep within a couple feet of him and dance the same shuffling step. On reaching the line of dancers behind him, he straightens his body and starts forward again; the line facing him retiring and the line behind him following. He waves a fly switch in his hand, and a string of njuga with pebbles inside is tied around his right ankle. On the last day, the patient eats a little fruit and delicacies for the benefit of the pepo.

The Razha warrior dance is performed by Arabs who brandish swords, bend their knees, and bow slightly in time with the beating of drums.

RAZHA: MILITARY AND WAR DANCE

The Razha was originally a war dance practiced by the Arabs in Arabia prior to starting out on a raid. It originated at Manga in Muscat (a section of Oman) and is danced with naked swords, the object being to strengthen the muscles of the sword arm. Hadramaut Arabs also dance it but use daggers instead of swords. A chapuo drum supplies the music for the Razha dance and a vumi drum is also beaten in the same manner as the chapuo.

The men stand in two rows facing each other, or in one row. They advance slowly, a few inches at each step, keeping time to the drumming. The sword is held perpendicularly in the right hand, the forearm being at a right angle with the body. While holding the hilt of the sword in a perfect balance between the thumb and the first and second fingers, the base of the hilt is given a smart blow with the wrist so as to make the blade of the sword quiver. Highly polished and made of fine, supple steel, the quivering blade reflects the light in a most effective manner. This can only be done with the long, straight, double-edged sword of southern Arabia and not with the scimitar-like blades that are often rattled together. In lieu of the cymbals, a metal rod is sometimes used, bent into a triangle.

The dancers move forward until they are about eight or ten paces apart. They bend the knee and bow the body slightly forward to each other in unison and in time to the beating of the drums.

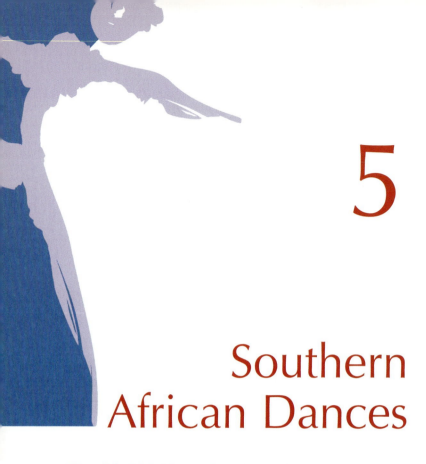

5

Southern
African Dances

The original inhabitants of southern Africa date back at least 20,000 years. They are now known as the San people. They were hunter-gatherers and made rock paintings throughout southern Africa. The oldest paintings (about 27,000 years old) are in Namibia. Others are in the Biggarsberg range of hills in South Africa and probably range in age between 4,000 years old and only a few centuries old. The pigments used for the paintings are red, white, and black. The red was made from ochre or iron oxide and is the most durable color. The paintings are always on the north or east sides of rock faces, perhaps to catch morning sunlight or because the good god traditionally lives in the east. The painters were probably shamans, as the paintings seem connected to trance healing dances. During these dances, the women and children would sit around the fire, clapping and singing, while the men danced in a circle. Some of the men

The San, who were renowned for their cave paintings like this one in Zimbabwe, were hunter-gatherers who were the first inhabitants of the Kalahari Desert region in southern Africa.

would enter a trance, and through the trance they had the power to take away illness.

JERUSAREMA: MILITARY AND SOCIAL DANCE

The Zezuru, who occupy the north-central part of Zimbabwe and constitute about one-fourth of all Shona-speaking people, traditionally dance the Jerusarema. Initially derived from a historical situation, the Jerusarema took on social and recreational characteristics through the years and is now preserved as a traditional dance. It is the nature of the oral tradition to produce a variety of choices and there are several versions of the origins of the Jerusarema dance.

The dance's original name, the Mbende, literally means "a mouse that runs fast." It acquired that name because of the rapid-striking movements made by the dancers upon hearing the music of the Jerusarema. Although the dance originated in the Zezuru area of Zimbabwe, it is now performed throughout the country thanks to a number of Jerusarema clubs. The Jerusarema may be danced at any time of the year, even during the time of planting and harvesting. Traditionally it is always danced in darkness, though usually not all night long, and it is always danced in open air in the middle of the village or township.

In response to the European colonists' prohibition of the dance in the 1800s, the Zezuru Council of Elders met to determine the best course of action to defend the dance that held such a sacred and historical place within their society. The chief was sent to the missionary who had proposed the ban to explain the dance's importance as a sacred celebration. When the chief arrived at the home of the missionary, he told him that he had dreamed of the "baby Jesus" of whom the missionary had frequently spoken. In the dream, the baby Jesus was being born and all the chiefs were going to Jerusalem to offer gifts and sing praise to the newborn child. In his dream, the chief said, he had also seen the Zezuru dancing and celebrating the birth of Jesus. This dance was a sacred dance that pleased all the holy men. The chief then explained to the missionary that he wanted his people to be allowed to perform the dance that he had dreamed of because it was a "divine" dance and they should be permitted to perform it to commemorate the birth of Jesus. Despite the chief's inaccuracy regarding the birthplace of Jesus, the missionary was impressed with his story and agreed that the dance should be performed.

Another version of the story proposed that the chief went to the missionary and told him that all significant events had to be commemorated by dance and music according to African tradition. He requested that his people be permitted to dance in celebration of Jesus Christ's birth. The request was granted and so the Mbende became the Jerusarema and the dance was saved. In effect, the Zezuru sacrificed the name so that they could continue to perform and participate in the dance.

The Jerusarema was developed as a diversionary tactic when the Shona warriors of the Zezuru tribe wanted to outwit their enemies. Its specific purpose was to distract the enemy and give the Shona warriors time to take up martial positions. Generally, the Zezuru's land was a high plateau and did not afford many natural obstructions. Therefore, the Zezuru created distractions out of their own resources, namely, women and music. In this way, the Mbende was born.

To achieve their objective, the Shona lined up a group of old men with timbers called mukwas that were made of rectangular bricks of wood and gave a high-pitched sound when struck together; ngomas, traditional drums; and hoshos, musical rattles made of gourds. When the men began playing the musical instruments, the women would run out onto the field and start dancing. Their hip-vibrating, waist-shaking movements ended with an accent on the pelvis, depicting sensual and beautiful distractions for the enemy. The women would repeat the movements as the old men gave the musical cues; the repetition itself could often become intoxicatingly hypnotic. While the women were out on the field dancing, the warriors gradually emerged from their compounds to take up their martial positions behind the lines of dancers and drummers. The dancers, in response to the approaching enemies, would grow more energetic in their movements, often teasing each other with competitive moves or being playful toward the drummers. All of this was designed to make the enemy think that the conquest would be easy, perhaps even pleasant. Once the Shona warriors had positioned themselves and the enemy had approached close enough to attack the dancers and drummers, an opening in the lines allowed a surprise attack on the enemy. Those too old or too young to fight were sometimes used in Mbende, since they would be perfect decoys.

Throughout the dance, movement never stops; the women clap their hands and the hosho players dance as they accompany the drums. The hosho players softly shift from side to side with gently bended knees and with their backs parallel to their bended knees. They then touch the adjacent player with their hips until it is time for them to make their dramatic pitch. The women make the same movements, except that they exaggerate the extension of their hips, resulting in the Umfundalai extension. This hyperextension is suspended each time the mukwas and ngomas cue them to begin their hip-shaking. The hosho player may be an older woman who does not dance but who presides over the correctness of the dance. She also ululates (only the women ululate), gauges the progress and tempo of the dance, and gives the cue for the women dancers to join in a chorus of ululations. She is a praise-giver: the ululation she performs can also be an indication of approval of some extraordinary feat of performance. When a dancer has danced very well, it is the sound of the trilling shrill that advises the dancer and spectators that a unique performance has occurred. Absence of the ululation puts an uncomfortable damper on the musicians and dancers.

Long after the threats of war had disappeared, the Mbende dance continued as a part of Shona celebrations and festivals. Europeans, who came to Shona territory in the nineteenth century, after the Matabele wave of invaders, represented the first seeds of colonialism in which both the Shona and Matabele would be subjugated.

Dance in Zimbabwe serves a number of roles and in those roles affirms and preserves the culture of the people. The interrelatedness of the social, political, and aesthetic aspects

Through its social, political, and aesthetic aspects, dance in Zimbabwe is a means to preserve the nation's culture.

of the dance allow it to be read as text for researchers and scholars who seek additional information about Zimbabwe culture and history.

KI-NYASA: HEALING DANCE

In Malawi, formerly known as Nyasaland, the village gets rid of an overabundance of animal spirits through the performance of the dance Ki-Nyasa. It is practiced only by men and women of humble origin and is danced in the open, either during the day or night. The animal spirits are removed by singing and running around in a circle, in time to drumming. The leader of the dance sings a solo and the others take up the chorus. The men wear a string of mjuga, which are strung around their knees, and stamp their foot at each step so as to make them jingle. A msondo drum is used—one end only is covered with goatskin—which is struck by the player's hands.

The open end of the drum rests on the ground, while the drummer stands astride the other end, which is supported by a cloth around his waist, and he plays in that position. The Ki-Nyasa has also been introduced to Zanzibar and coastal sections of East Africa.

RELIGIOUS AND SPIRITUAL DANCES

The Banda is a Cewa tribal dance from Malawi that is performed in a ceremony to worship Gede, the god of cemeteries and of reproduction. The dance symbolizes death and life, as well as the celebration of the future and the past in the present moment. Chiwoda is a very popular Malawian dance that is performed by women at funerals and festivals.

MIDIMU MASK DANCE

The Midimu (mask dancers), who are from the Makonde tribe of southern Tanzania and Mozambique, dance during the rites of boys and girls coming out of their respective initiation camps. For three consecutive days there is joy, feasting, and dancing. After the boys and girls have been officially accepted into society as adults and sent home to their parents by the chief or clan leader, the Midimu sponsors disperse into their respective groups to follow the new members of society. They make systematic rounds to every home where there is an initiate and dance there for some time before moving on to another. By evening, they retire to their homes. During the two days that follow, they either repeat performances at the same houses or go to new places. The member of the family who has a girl or boy initiate gives gifts to the dancers. After three days of performance, the Midimu disappear and will not reappear until another initiation season, which could be three years or more.

It is obvious that the Midimu are essentially pieces of art; part and parcel of the initiation rituals of transition for boys and girls. They are a tool for the demonstration of the social importance that society attaches to the change of status among its members: the justification of the rigorous activities they underwent in camp; a social get-together to rejoice with the initiating parents; a theatrical entertainment; and a form of social organization. Mask dancing has been commercialized in certain quarters and has become part entertainment due to changes in people's way of life. In their strict traditional context, Midimu perform only at occasions of initiation. The form in which the Midimu appear is mystical (women and children are not supposed to know that men dance the masks). At the same time, they reveal that initiated men have power to control these mysteries. Midimu, in this case, are visual aids to teach society the proper place of both initiated and uninitiated men and women. For that reason, Midimu contribute toward character building, consciousness of position, and the duties and responsibilities such positions carry. They are a means of teaching good citizenship and intensify the bonds of social organization.

The Mozambique Makonde Midimu mask is much like a helmet, covering the entire head and worn at an angle, slanting backwards to allow air circulation through the neck end of the mask, the mouth, eyes, and, of course, the nostrils. The dancer performs for almost half a day and precautions are taken against suffocation. The Midimu dancer wears a tightly fitting costume of long pants and a long-sleeved shirt. Over this he wears a net-like tunic made from strings and small bells over the tunic. His helmet-mask has cloth stitched to its bottom, which is left to fall loosely over the shoulders.

Five drums, a rattle, and two pairs of singers are used to accompany the dance. The crowd, including women and children, functions as the chorus. Midimu songs are sung in Makonde (even when the Yao tribe of Malawi perform them as part of their Midimu ritual). The Mozambican Makonde mask dancer is a typical case of high-class dramatization, though movements in the dances of different songs are usually standard.

MOHOBELO: HARVEST DANCE

Mohobelo from the Sotho people of South Africa is a rain dance performed by men and women after the dry winter season. Black and khaki trousers, shoes, and some sort of headdress with short black ostrich feathers are worn with a blanket casually thrown over the shoulders. Great strides and leaps characterize this dance.

MILITARY AND WAR DANCES

The people of Lesotho perform the Mokhibo, which is danced entirely on the knees by women and children, while the men perform their Mokorotlo. The dancers clap their hands and make high-pitched trilling sounds called molilietsane. Mokorotlo is a war dance performed by men. The men recite the praises of their warrior ancestors. The dance entails the swinging of the body and rhythmic stomping of the feet. Often, a man will break away from the group and kick his feet high in the air.

Inzumba is a Tswa (Mozambique) dance originally performed by males and females for their neighboring allies, the Tongo. This dance uses half a dozen xylophones and drums, and the song "Timbila" is sung. The Tswa is a step dance performed in a semi-circle in which dancers tie a number of rattles onto one leg below the knee and perform a series of swift steps.

INCWALA: ANCIENT COURT DANCE

Incwala is a Swazi ritual dance performed by men and women that illustrates the responsibilities of a king. A king must be strong and lead his people, but he must also be compassionate. Cattle, the most prized possession of the Swazi people, traditionally must be present at the ritual. The king, known as the lion (*Ngwenyama*), shares his power with his mother, an elephant (*Ndlovukati*), and is praised as the lion, the bull, and the great mountain. Special dignitaries offer water that has been collected from all over the country and plants from the forest. This dance is performed at the first new moon of the year.

SOCIAL AND CEREMONIAL DANCES

Ukukanya nganya is a dance that is part of the many rituals in preparation for wedding and marriage. Three weeks after the groom's mothers have visited the bride, the groom and his friends come over to bring cattle. The groom and his friends perform the stomping dance, or Ukukanya nganya. The bride, her mothers, and companions dance at the same time in a separate group; one mother carrying the bride on her shoulders. The men wear long garments and carry spears in their hands.

Ukwingesia is a ritual washing that the bride goes through in preparation for her wedding and marriage. During this ritual, the groom's mothers and girlfriends of the bride perform a dance. The purpose of the entire ritual—which is at the same time a puberty ritual—is to protect the physical and mental health of the girl and to ensure her fertility. Medicines are administered several times during the ritual and her mothers instruct the bride and mothers-in-law regarding proper conduct as a wife and mother. The bride is carried first by one and then another of her "mothers," while the other mothers and young women, with the bride raised high in their midst, dance back and forth. All the while, the bride holds a mat to shield her head and face. After about five minutes, there is a short break during which the bride's mothers formally greets the mothers-in-law and receives gifts. Then the groom's mothers dance again.

The Ngoma is a round dance. It is a Nyasa social and recreational dance that is performed in the mines and the men sometimes dress up like women to perform the dance. They wave ox tails and handkerchiefs as they dance.

Maribotu is a Chopi hunting dance from Mozambique in which the men are dressed in lion skins, ornamented with monkey tails. Warriors carry spears and large oval shields.

Women and children of the Ndebele people of southern Zimbabwe and northern South Africa accompany the Muchongoyo dance which is also known as the "hunting dance" in that it captures movements during and after the hunt.

Makwaya is a Shangaan dance from Mozambique that is performed by men with a great deal of miming. The men wear a white uniform with white trousers and a white vest embroidered with different symbols such as cattle, birds, trees, and names. The men sing a song called "Fanakalo."

Mutshongolo is a recreational stomping dance of South Africa that is performed by men, while they brandish shields; however, it is not a fighting or war dance. Some of the movements are pointing actions with sticks and shields called *muthlokozo*, quick stamping action called *kutshongolo*, swaying of shields known as *kuswaya*, and smacking of shields with sticks known as *kuba sithlango*.

The Ndulumu dance is a secular dance performed by men for pleasure and entertainment in Swaziland. The men wear a calfskin apron-like garment and sing a song called the

"Mntaka NoMenza Hemu." The dance is performed in a single or double line and is done in sequence with the singing. The Ndulumu is breathtaking when performed with hundreds of men.

The Muchongoyo is a southern Zimbabwean dance performed by men of the Ndebele people. It is danced for recreational and social purposes and is known for its characteristic high leg lifts and propulsive stomps. Women are mainly used as musicians who play the hoshos and sing alongside the men. The women move while singing, shuffling from side to side without lifting their feet and putting their hands to their foreheads in alternation. The drums accompany the dance and whistles are blown as an accent to the stomps.

Isicathulo, commonly known as the boot dance, was originally performed at a mission when dancing was outlawed and it was a form of protest. Now it is a South African dance performed in boots. Men traditionally dance Isicathulo, but when women dance it, they dress as men.

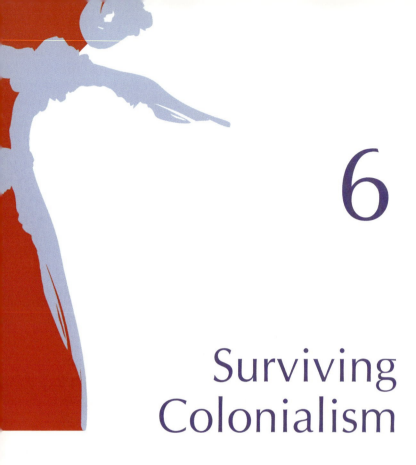

6

Surviving Colonialism

European philosophy, aesthetics, and religious attitudes became stamped on the cultures of Africans in the early-to mid-nineteenth century. As hard and fast as the European stamp tended to be, it was not an indelible or penetrating one. European dress and languages, and the reality of native commissioners and missionaries, did not totally obliterate African culture. In many cases, specially created laws enforced the adoption and adaptation of European cultural behaviors. The colonialists enlisted the help of the law in forcing Africans to abandon traditional practices and embrace European ones. There were laws that forbade dancing on Sundays and there were laws that designated what dances and music could be played and on which occasions. These restrictions served to drive many traditions underground and/or create new and veiled meanings that would be satisfactory to the colonial governors and missionaries.

Bono, of the Irish rock group U2, dances with an AIDS orphan in Uganda.

African villagers continued to treat their chiefs as their rulers and to worship their gods, even though there were now native commissioners and the God of the missionaries. As representatives of European "civilization and morality," the missionaries were not only spokesmen for their God but keepers of European culture as well. To many missionaries, the dances of Africans were lustful, indecent, and provocative. Campaigns to outlaw and prohibit certain dances were common and often were pursued with evangelical zeal.

The introduction of Christianity into Africa had emasculating consequences on many forms of dance. Europeans recognized that dance was intertwined with indigenous religion and morality; and so, even though African dances have themes and origins comparable to those of European folk dances, their performances were seen as the manifestation of savage heathenism and were antagonistic to the "true faith." African dance was found to be too licentious for the civilized Victorian Europeans. This represented a classic clash of cultures. Unfortunately for Africans, the power for change was on the other side. Hip-gyrations of any sort were antithetical to the visiting Europeans for whom the hips maintained an almost immobile link with the human torso. It was a cultural misunderstanding and refusal by the missionaries to interpret properly what they were observing. The dances were definitely energetic, sensual, and physical, but they were hardly the orgiastic events that the colonialists portrayed.

Missionaries often were able to convince native commissioners that "lustful" dances should be prohibited as hindrances to Christianity and civilization. This observation highlights two items of interest: First, many Africans, despite being Christianized, always incorporated their own traditions with the newly imposed European ones. Second, Africans attending church and then returning to the village to dance was an acknowledgement of old and newly acquired belief systems. This was part of a survival tactic that would be employed over and over again to save their earlier traditions.

As you have read throughout this book, African dance has had to undergo a myriad of changes largely due to colonialism and war mandates. It has managed to survive and, indeed, triumph. Many African dances parallel the development and histories of the countries they represent. Attempts to legislate,

Not just a religious and social expression, African dance can also be a political expression. Here delegates from Zimbabwe's ZANU Party dance in support of their president, Robert Mugabe, in 2002.

ban, or modify the dances have largely been unsuccessful. From the Baladi dances in North Africa to the Jerusarema dance in southern Africa, the will and determination to dance is indicative of the spirit of millions of Africans.

The Jerusarema is an excellent example of a historical dance. It documents a tactic of war and is danced by people with a deep sense of pride and perseverance. Although not technically a war dance in as much as the dancers are not enacting a war scene or demonstrating preparation for war, the Jerusarema is in effect a military drill, albeit one of distraction, diversion, and disguise. The combatants who participated in the seven-year war to overthrow the ruling white government of Rhodesia, and help create the nation of Zimbabwe, danced the Jerusarema as a symbolic gesture of their military strength and

Then-South African President Nelson Mandela dances at his country's Freedom Day celebrations in 1999.

nationalistic pride as well as a demonstration of their collective survival skills. Its beauty, vibrancy, and energy made the Jerusarema a therapeutic dance for many war-weary and exhausted combatants. It became a symbol of hope and a source of connectedness that foretold unity with their families and friends. Today it is a national dance having transcended its ethnicity to become a dance that all Zimbabweans embrace and proclaim as belonging to them.

In Africa, dance is a social, political, and religious construct that impacts all institutions in society. The pervasive quality of dance is indicative of its importance to African culture. The ability of the dance to reflect the society's image both morally and aesthetically is integral to many African dance forms. African dance is representative of the society as a whole as it often embraces and addresses the issues and concerns of that society.

aimo Disease that is caused by being possessed by a demon.

akamba Term for demons that possess people; they can be driven away by Kilumi dance and song.

alma Egyptian word for a woman of learning.

asa or **asaya** A thick, solid bamboo staff carried by Egyptian men. It was used in the Tahtib dance, which was both a form of recreation and a martial art. This staff, also known as shoum or nabboot, was carried on long journeys, especially at night.

banja Rhythm sticks used by the Twa people in the Molimo songs and dance.

Bes An ancient Egyptian god, at whose festivals dancing and tambourine playing were featured.

chapuo A drum used in many North African dances, such as Shebwani, Ngoma ya Fimbo, Razha, and Chama. It is 18 inches long, 8 in diameter, and is covered with goatskin on both ends. It is hung across the waist of the drummer by a cord about the neck and is played with the hands on both ends.

dawa An herbal medicine administered by a fundi to make the pepo speak.

fundi An elderly Swahili man or woman who specializes in the professional exorcising of pepo. Also known as a mganga.

gour A Nubian term for an evil spirit. It can be dealt with through a Zar ceremony.

iblis A Nubian term for an evil spirit. It can be dealt with through a Zar ceremony.

jalabeya A white gown worn by the patient at a Zar ceremony.

jinn An Arabic term for an evil spirit. It can be dealt with through a Zar ceremony.

kinanda A string instrument of the nature of a guitar. It usually has seven strings, six of which were formerly made of sheep gut but are now made of twisted silk. The seventh is the bass string and is made of copper wire.

kithembe Cylindrical drum covered at one end (the top side) with goatskin known as Kithuma kya mbui. It is played with both hands; the drum is slanted and held between the knees. The Kithembe drum is used in Kilumi music and dance.

kotola iito Rolling shoulder movement used in the Ngoma/Mwase dance and music tradition.

krotalistria Ancient Egyptian term for a specialist in dancing with castanets.

kuba sithlango Smacking of shields with sticks used in the South African stomping dance Mutshongolo.

kuswaya Swaying of shields used in the South African stomping dance Mutshongolo.

kutshongolo Quick stamping action used in the South African stomping dance Mutshongolo.

maharuma A bedouin headdress worn during the Pepo ya ki-arabu dance ceremony.

makata Sticks cut to different lengths and tuned to different pitches, used by the Babira people of Congo to make the complicated rhythms of the Nkumbi dance.

marwasi A treble drum used in the Shebwani and Kinanda dances. It measures 8 inches long by 8 inches in diameter. It is covered with goatskin on both ends and is beaten with the flat of the right hand while held in the left with a piece of cord.

mazmar An oboe-type woodwind used in Egyptian Baladi.

mbibi A single or double flute/pipe used to provide music for Ncungo dance.

mentis A religious instrument of ancient Egypt. Women in harems might learn to play this instrument.

mganga An elderly Swahili man or woman who specializes in the professional exorcising of pepo. Also known as a fundi.

mikanda Drums used to accompany the Nzaiko ya Ngingo initiation dance. Only during the dance may these drums be used in the initiation.

mikathi Ankle bells made of pellet bells tied together. Used for dancing in the Authi dance.

mjuga or **njuga** A string of small iron bells worn by the men who dance the Ki-Nyasa. The mjuga is worn at the knee and jingles when the foot is stamped. Njuga are also used in pepo dances.

msondo A large drum used in the dances Ki-Nyasa, Sherha, and Mdema. It measures about six 6 in length by 12 to 15 inches in diameter. One end is covered with goatskin, which is struck with the player's hands. The open end of the drum rests on the ground, while the drummer stands astride the other end, which is supported by a cloth around his waist, and he plays in that position. The msondo drum is rather high-pitched for its size.

mukanda The drum used to accompany Mwase dance.

muthlokozo Pointing actions with stick and shield used in the South African stomping dance Mutshongolo.

nai A flute used in Egyptian Baladi.

ncuguma A piece of carved stick beaten against a flat board to produce a rattling sound. Used in Authi dance.

ndlovukati A Swazi term for the king's mother, meaning "the elephant."

ngutha A type of drum used for Ncungo dance. Three or four drums are used.

Ngwenyama A Swazi term for the king, literally meaning "the lion."

ntoyi A master drum that is played by hand rather than with sticks. It is used in the Sindimba dance.

Nyikang Nubian term for the collective ongoing existence of ancestors as well as the power of a higher, supernatural force.

nzaiko nene The great circumcision initiation rite.

orchestria Ancient Egyptian term for dancer.

pepo A Swahili term for an evil spirit. It is dealt with through the various pepo dances.

Reth Nubian term for king.

sagaat Small finger cymbals used in Egyptian Baladi.

shantan afrit A Nubian term for an evil spirit. It can be dealt with through a Zar ceremony.

shumburere A hat with a tall, conical crown and a very wide brim. It is woven from the split fronds of the dom palm or the mkindu palm, the wild date. From the outer edge of the brim is suspended a fringe composed of strips of colored cloth, which hang down to the pit of the stomach in front and to the same level at the back. The shumburere is worn in some pepo dances.

sistra A religious instrument of ancient Egypt. Women in harems might learn to play this instrument.

tarha A white veil worn by the patient at a Zar ceremony.

tari or **pari** A tambourine used in dances such as Mwasha, pepo, and Chama. A tari is sometimes ornamented with loose brass discs that jingle together as in the Spanish tambourine. The goatskin is pegged to the wooden frame and is tightened by stuffing a thick cord between the skin and the frame.

torosi A leather breast and back plate connected by straps over the shoulders, profusely decorated with beads and cowrie shells. Used in some pepo dances.

ud A lute used in Egyptian Baladi.

udi A scented wood that is made into a paste for some of the pepo dances.

vitasa Brass cymbals used in the North African dances Shebwani, Ngoma ya Fimbo, and Chama.

vumi A bass drum used in North African dances such as Shebwani, Sherha, Razha, Chama, pepo dances, and Ngoma ya Fimbo. It is 2 to 3 feet long, 15 inches in diameter, and is covered with goatskin on both ends. It is hung across the waist of the drummer by a cord about the neck, and is played with the hands on both ends.

zar A Nubian term for an evil spirit. It can be dealt with through a Zar ceremony.

zumari A clarinet used in North African dances such as Ngoma ya Fimbo, Chama, and Sherha.

African Carving: a Dogon Kanaga Mask. Directed by Eliot Elisofon and Thomas Blakely. The Film Study Center of Harvard University, 1975.

Beauty and the Beast: Two Igbo Masquerades. Produced by Herbert M. Cole. African Studies Program in the Jackson School of International Studies, University of Washington, 1985.

Behind the Mask. Produced by BBC-TV and Warner Bros, 1976. (Dogon people of Mali).

Chuck Davis, Dancing through West Africa. Produced by Gorham Kindem and Jane Desmond, 1987. (Native dance traditions of Senegal and Gambia).

Dances of Egypt. Produced by Aisha Ali, 1991.

Dances of North Africa, Vol. I. Produced by Aisha Ali.

Dances of Southern Africa. Produced, directed, and photographed by Gei Zantzinger. Media Sales, Pennsylvania State University, 1973.

Discovering the Music of Africa. Directed by Bernard Wilets, 1994.

Efe: Gelede Ceremonies among the Western Yoruba. Produced by Henry John Drewal, 1992.

Egypt Dances. Produced by Magda Saleh. William Patterson College TV, 1980.

Folk Dances of Egypt and the Sudan. Edited by Mahmoud Reda. Middle Eastern Television Productions, 1984.

Herdsmen of the Sun. Directed by Werner Herzog, 1988. (Wodaabe Tribe).

Ndebele Women and the Rituals of Rebellion. Directed by Peter Rich, 1995.

Way of the Wodaabe. Produced by Kevin A. Peer. National Geographic Explorer, 1988.

Yoruba Performance. Produced by John Drewal, 1991.

African Dance Resources
www.artslynx.org/dance/afro.htm

African Dance Groups
**http://dir.yahoo.com/Arts/Performing_Arts/Dance/
Folk_and_Traditional/African/Groups/**

African Dance and Drum Classes, Tribal Music,
and African-American Art
www.ethnicarts.org

West African Dance Workshop
www.ga.k12.pa.us/academics/ls/3/Africa/dance/dance.htm

AfriCan Dance Conference
www.griots.net/archives/focus/dance.html

African Dance Tradition and Philosophy
http://umfundalai.com

West African Dance Classes Taught By Youssouf Koumbassa
www.westafricandance.com

Bibliography

Asiama, Simeon D. "Abofoo: A Study of Akan Hunters' Music." Ph.D. diss., Wesleyan University, 1977.

Duodu, E.A. "Drumming and Dancing in Akan Society." Master's thesis, Wesleyan University, 1972, 108.

Jahn, Janheinz. *Muntu: African Culture and the Western World.* New York: Grove Weidenfeld, 1990.

Nketia, J.H. *The Music of Africa.* New York: W.W. Norton & Company, 1974.

———. *Drumming in Akan Communities of Ghana.* Edinburgh: Thomas Nelson & Sons, 1963, 205.

Opoku, A.M. "African Dance." *International Encyclopedia of Dance.* New York: Oxford University Press (Unedited version).

———. "The Dance Ensemble" (Institute of African Studies 1967).

———. "Dances of the Secret Society." *International Journal of African Dance* 1, no. 1. Edited by Kariamu Welsh Asante, Institute for African Dance Research and Performance, Temple University, Philadelphia, Pa., 1992.

Thompson, Robert Farris. *African Art in Motion.* Los Angeles: University of California Press, 1974.

Welsh Asante, Kariamu. "The Aesthetic Conceptualization of Nzuri." *The African Aesthetic: Keeper of the Traditions.* Westport, Conn.: Greenwood Press, 1993.

———. "Commonalities in African Dance." *African Culture: The Rhythms of Unity.* Edited by Molefi Kete Asante and Kariamu Welsh Asante. Trenton, N.J.: African World Press, 1990.

Asante, Molefi Kete. *African Culture: The Rhythms of Unity*. Edited by Kariamu Welsh Asante and Mike Ashley. Trenton, N.J.: Africa World Press, 1989.

Collins, John. *West African Pop Roots*. Philadelphia, Pa.: Temple University Press, 1992.

Nketia, J.H. Kwabena. *The Music of Africa*. New York: W.W. Norton & Co., 1974.

Price, Christine. *Talking Drums of Africa*. New York: Charles Scribner's, 1973.

Welsh Asante, Kariamu, ed. *The African Aesthetic: Keeper of the Traditions*. Westport, Conn.: Praeger Press, 1994.

———. *African Dance*. Trenton, N.J.: Africa World Press, 1994.

———. *African Dance: An Artistic, Historical, and Philosophical Inquiry*. Edited by Kariamu Welsh Asante. Trenton, N.J.: Africa World Press, 1996.

———. *Zimbabwe Dance: Rhythmic Forces, Ancestral Voices, and Aesthetic Analysis*. Trenton, N.J.: Africa World Press, 2000.

Index

Index

Index

Index

Kariamu Welsh, a professor of dance in the Esther Boyer School of Music and Department of Dance at Temple University, received her Doctor of Arts from New York University and her MA.H. from the State University of New York at Buffalo. Dr. Welsh is widely published in both scholarly journals and book-length studies, and is a scholar of cultural studies including performance and culture within Africa and the African Diaspora. Dr. Welsh serves as the Director of the Institute for African Dance Research and Performance. She is the author of two recently published books by Africa World Press, Trenton, N.J.: *Zimbabwe Dance: Rhythmic Forces, Ancestral Voices and Aesthetic Analysis* and *Umfundalai: An African Dance Technique.* She is the editor of *The African Aesthetic: Keeper of the Traditions* (Praeger Press, 1994) and *African Dance: An Artistic, Historical and Philosophical Inquiry* (Africa World Press, 1996). She coedited *African Culture: Rhythms of Unity* (Africa World Press, 1985). Dr. Welsh is the artistic director of Kariamu & Co.: Traditions, and is the recipient of numerous fellowships, grants, and awards including a National Endowment for the Arts Choreography Fellowship, the Creative Public Service Award of New York, a 1997 Pew Fellowship, a 1997 Simon Guggenheim Fellowship, a 1998 Pennsylvania Council on the Arts grant, and three Senior Fulbright Scholar Awards. She is the founding artistic director of the National Dance Company of Zimbabwe in southern Africa. Dr. Welsh is the creator of the Umfundalai dance technique, a Pan-African contemporary technique that has been in existence for more than 33 years.